A

# English Bu

## Commercial Correspondence for Foreign Students
## NEW EDITION

## F. W. King F.I.L. (Ger.)
## D. Ann Cree

Revised by David O'Gorman

LONGMAN

**LONGMAN GROUP LIMITED**
Longman House, Burnt Mill, Harlow,
Essex CM20 2JE, England
*and Associated Companies throughout the world.*

First published 1962
Second edition 1979
Fifth impression 1984
ISBN 0 582 55353 9


Printed in Singapore by
Huntsmen Offset Printing Pte Ltd

## Acknowledgements

We are grateful to the following for permission
to reproduce copyright material:

Barnaby's Picture Library for page 57 (bottom
left); British Airways for page 90; British Rail-
ways Board for page 84; Furness Withy Group
for page 86; Keystone Press Agency Ltd., for
page 56 (middle bottom); Libreria Britanica S.A.
for page 38; Lloyds Bank Ltd., for page 107;
Lloyd's of London for pages 124 & 125.

We have been unable to trace the copyright
holder of the photograph on page 57 (bottom
right), and would be grateful for any information
that would enable us to do so.

# Contents

# Introduction

The English language has often been described as a 'living' language. This means that it grows and renews itself by a never-ending process of taking up new words and expressions and pushing worn-out ones into the background to languish or die. The process is slow: each age adds something to the national heritage, something that is typical of the spirit of that age. The result is clearly seen in the writing and speech of that age.

In compiling this work on Business English we had in mind chiefly the need of the foreign student of English who has mastered basic grammar and acquired a fair vocabulary and some idiom, and who now wishes to apply his knowledge to the study of business letter writing. We have therefore given examples of letters written in a clear, direct, friendly and positive style. (We have also kept in mind the need of the student who requires English for correspondence with English-speaking countries, and whose interest therefore lies mainly in import-export matters.)

In this new edition we have given 150 specimen letters as well as some 740 phrases and extracts from letters. No book of commercial correspondence could reproduce specimen letters in every style of expression used in commercial writing, but the carefully classified groups of phrases given will enable the student to build his own letters on the pattern of the specimens.

In this edition many of the letters are presented in a more attractive and realistic style and the revisions have also taken into account decimalisation and metrication.

We think these revisions will make our book even more useful as a guide to business letter writing.

F. W. KING
D. ANN CREE

# 1 | Business letter writing

Letter-writing is an essential part of business. In spite of telephone, telex and telegraphic communication the writing of letters continues; in fact most telephoned and telegraphed communications have to be confirmed in writing.

The letter is often evidence of an arrangement or a contract, and must therefore be written with care; even the shortest and most usual of letters may have this importance. The need for thought in writing is clear when you realise that in speaking—either face-to-face or by telephone—the reaction to the spoken word can be seen or heard immediately, but reaction to a letter is not known until the answer is received.

When you have written a letter, read it through carefully; see that you have put in everything you intended, and have expressed it well; read it again, trying to put yourself in the place of the receiver, to find out what impression your letter will make.

It is obvious that what has been said in the previous paragraph becomes even more important when you write a letter in a foreign language. Unless you know that particular language very well you are certain to translate some phrases from your own language literally; these phrases may then convey quite a different meaning from that intended. It is in any case impossible to translate all business phrases literally as each language has its own characteristic idiom. With this in mind we have given as large a selection as possible of English phrases in general use.

A question frequently asked is: 'How long should a good letter be?' The answer is: 'As long as is necessary to say what has to be said.' The manner of interpreting this varies, of course, with the writer, and also very greatly with the nationality of the writer.

Because the aim of the letter is to secure the interest of the reader, and his co-operation, the letter should begin with sentences that will introduce the matter without undue delay, and polite forms to help the introduction must not be too long. The letter should continue with the subject itself and all the necessary information or arguments connected with it, but the wording must carry the reader along smoothly; jerky, over-short or disjointed sentences spoil the impression. The letter should have a suitable ending—one that is not long but makes the reader feel that his point of view is being considered. This is especially necessary when sellers are writing to buyers.

Waste of time in subsequent letters should be avoided by giving all the information likely to be required, unless the writer purposely refrains from going into too much detail until he knows the reaction of his correspondent.

A good vocabulary is necessary, both in your own and foreign languages; repetition should be avoided as much as possible, except where the exact meaning does not allow any change of word.

Everyone has a characteristic way of writing, but it must be remembered that the subject of the routine business letter lacks variety and certain accepted phrases are in general use. This is of great help to the foreigner, who can rely on them to compose a letter that will be understood. Let us say, perhaps, that a routine business letter is like a train, running on a railway track, whereas other letters are like cars that must, of course, keep to the road but are otherwise given greater freedom of movement than a train.

This greater 'freedom of movement' applies also to business correspondence dealing with matters of policy, special offers, negotiations, reports and customers' complaints, all of which are matters that demand individual treatment. Here the correspondent must not only make his meaning clear but also try to create in the reader's imagination a true impression of his attitude. This is by no means so difficult as it may seem if the writer will remember that simplicity of word and phrase usually gives the impression of sincerity. Also a style of writing which is natural to the writer carries his personality to the reader.

In foreign trade, with its numerous problems and complications, the use of forms is a necessity: it facilitates the handling of goods at the various stages, indicates that regulations have been complied with, and saves unnecessary correspondence. It is the repetitive nature of many business transactions that makes it possible for the form to do the work of the letter. A study of the wording on forms is therefore advisable, and one or two specimens relating to certain transactions will be found in later chapters.

The growing use of the telephone and telegraph is also reducing correspondence in this age when, as never before, 'time is money'. Another factor is the increasing personal contact in international trade. With any one part of the world only a few hours' flying time from any other it is not surprising that many businessmen prefer to make personal visits in order to discuss important matters on the spot.

Other modern conditions and tendencies that have their effect on the nature of correspondence are the establishment of foreign companies by large international organisations, business tie-ups between pairs of firms in different countries, export and import controls and restrictions, currency controls and the financial policies of governments.

The really competent correspondent therefore needs to understand something of the principles and practice of modern commerce. There is no room in this book for even an outline of these principles, but some brief explanations of certain procedures are given in order to help the less experienced student to understand the letters that follow.

# 2 | The letter heading and the layout

Business letters are usually typed on notepaper bearing a specially designed heading which provides the reader of the letter with essential information about the organisation sending it. Normally the heading will include the company's name and address, its telephone numbers and telegraphic addresses, the type of business it is engaged in, its telex code and V.A.T.[1] number, and in many cases the names of the directors. It is becoming increasingly common for firms to print an emblem or trademark on their stationery.

Here is an example of a heading that might be used by a British company:

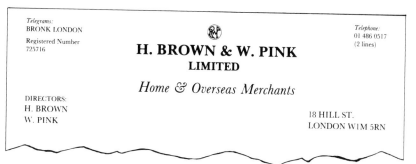

*Telegrams:*
BRONK LONDON
Registered Number
725716

**H. BROWN & W. PINK**
**LIMITED**

*Home & Overseas Merchants*

*Telephone:*
01 486 0517
(2 lines)

DIRECTORS:
H. BROWN
W. PINK

18 HILL ST.
LONDON W1M 5RN

The firm in this example is a *limited company*,[2] and this fact is indicated by the word 'Limited' (very often abbreviated to 'Ltd.'), which is printed after the name. Since the name of the company does not show what its line of business is, this is stated separately.

Here are two more examples of letter headings, both of which would be used by *partnerships*.[2]

## GREY, BLACK & WHITE

SOLICITORS

*Telephone:* 01 388 5599

T.M. White
G.R. Jones

265 HIGH HOLBORN
LONDON WC1H 8BA

[1] Value Added Tax, an indirect tax which replaced Purchase Tax in connection with Britain's entry into the European Economic Community (the E.E.C.).   [2] See page 8.

Let us now look at an example of a letter typed on the stationery of a British limited company:

(a) Telegrams
GRAJO LEEDS

# GRADEN & JONES
## LIMITED

*Home & Overseas Merchants*

Telephone
Leeds 978653

DIRECTORS:
L.L. Graden, P.G. Jones

Upper Bridge Street
LEEDS 2

(b) JAS/DS

(c)    13 July 1978

(d) Oliver Green and Co. Ltd.
25 King Edward VII St.
MANCHESTER M24 5BD

(e) Dear Sirs

We understand from several of our trade connections in Bolton that you are the British agents for Petrou and Galitopoulos AE of Athens.

Will you please send us price-lists and catalogues for all products manufactured by this company, together with details of trade discounts and terms of payment.

We look forward to hearing from you.

(f) Yours faithfully
GRADEN AND JONES LTD.

(g)    *J.A. Stevens*

J.A. Stevens
Chief Buyer

Note the layout in the example. Currently there are several ways of setting out a business letter in Britain, and policy in this respect differs

4

from company to company. The form in which a business letter appears has not been standardised in the United Kingdom to the extent it has in the U.S.A. and most European countries, and many British firms still indent the first line of each paragraph, and use more punctuation in the inside name and address and in the date than is the case in our example. Nevertheless there is a growing tendency in Britain, due largely to foreign influences and the widespread use of the electric typewriter, to use block paragraphing—in other words, to begin every line at the left-hand margin—and to dispense with unnecessary punctuation in the date and the name and address of the person or organisation written to. It is still considered necessary to put a full stop after abbreviations, as we have done in the case of *Co.* (Company), *Ltd.* (Limited) and *St.* (Street) in our example. However, it is becoming more and more common to type *Mr* and *Mrs*—i.e. without a stop—and this practice may well be extended to other abbreviations in the near future.

*The parts of the letter*
(*a*) *The heading*. This has already been mentioned. Note that this example, like the one on page 3, contains all the information mentioned in the first paragraph of this chapter.
(*b*) *The reference*. This is typed on the same line as the date, but on the left, and consists of the initials of the person who signs the letter (in this case JAS) and those of the typist (DS). Sometimes other initials or figures are added, according to whatever may suit the filing system of the firm in question. It is usual to quote the reference initials of the addressee company in a reply.
(*c*) *The date*. The form in which the date is written in this letter—13 July 1978—is probably the simplest and clearest of all the current forms used in the English-speaking world, but there are alternative ways of writing the date, for example:

July 13 1978 (Americans put the name of the month first),
13th July 1978, and
July 13th 1978.

Some firms still insist on a comma before the year, but others consider this unnecessary. It is important to note that the name of the town or city where the letter originates is *not* repeated before the date, although this is normally done on the Continent. Another practice widely used in Europe is to write the date in a highly abbreviated form—12.7.78, for example—but this should not be done in letters written in English, since in Britain 12.7.78 means 12 July 1978, whereas in the U.S.A. it means December 7 1978. It is obvious that the use of such forms could result in confusion.
(*d*) *The inside address*. A few points concerning the name and address

of the firm written to need to be made. Firstly, they are typed on the left, normally against the margin. The diagonal grading of the name and address is rare nowadays, and the style shown in the example is neater, as well as being quicker for the typist.

Secondly, the use of *Messrs.* (an abbreviated form of *Messieurs*, the French word for *Gentlemen*) should not be used in front of the name of a limited company, nor should it appear with the names of firms which indicate their line of business and do not consist of family names. It follows, therefore, that *Messrs.* will be used mostly when a partnership is being addressed, as in this example:

Messrs. Hamilton and Jacobs
265 High Holborn
London WC1 7GS

Note also that the number of the street in the address always precedes the name of the street, and that in the case of large towns and cities in the United Kingdom the name of the county is not required. It is not necessary, for example, to add 'Lancashire' to the address in the example on page 4. However, when the firm addressed is situated in a smaller town, the county name is necessary, and it should be remembered that in Britain there are two Richmonds, one in Surrey and another in Yorkshire, and several Newports, for example.

(e) *The salutation.*    Below the address a double space at least is left, and the words 'Dear Sirs' are typed. This is the usual *salutation* in British business letters addressed to a company rather than to an individual within the company. Very often a comma is typed after the salutation, but an increasing number of firms are eliminating this, considering the spacing to fulfil the function of traditional punctuation. Once again, there are no hard-and-fast 'rules', but every firm will have its own policy. In the U.S.A. the most common salutation is 'Gentlemen:'. Note that the salutation is typed against the left-hand margin.

When writing to an individual within the firm addressed, the salutation is 'Dear Sir' ('Dear Madam' if the recipient is known to be a woman), or 'Dear Mr_____', 'Dear Mrs_____', 'Dear Miss_____' or 'Dear Ms_____' if the addressee is addressed by name rather than by position.

In recent years the use of the form *Ms* has become quite common. It originated in the U.S.A. and, like its 'male' equivalent *Mr*, it does not indicate whether the person addressed is married or unmarried.

(f) *The complimentary close.*    This is typed above the name of the firm sending the letter, then a space is left for the signature. If the salutation is 'Dear Sirs' or 'Dear Sir', the complimentary close will read 'Yours faithfully' or, less commonly, 'Yours truly'. If the correspondent is addressed by his or her name—'Dear Mr Brown', 'Dear Miss James', etc.—the complimentary close will take the form 'Yours sincerely'.

Here are some examples:

| Name and address | Salutation | Complimentary close |
| --- | --- | --- |
| Southern Airways Ltd.<br>250 Oxford Street<br>London W1 7TM | Dear Sirs | Yours faithfully<br>(Yours truly) |
| The Marketing Manager<br>Software Ltd.<br>Richmond<br>Surrey SFY 3DF | Dear Sir | Yours faithfully<br>(Yours truly) |
| Ms J. Faulkner<br>British Films Ltd.<br>3 Wardour St.<br>London W1 5JN | Dear Ms Faulkner | Yours sincerely |

(g) *The signature.* It often happens that the person who has dictated a letter is unable to sign it as soon as it has been typed. Since it is often essential to send a letter as soon as possible, the typist or some other employee connected with the letter in question will sign it instead: in such cases he or she will write the word 'for' or the initials 'p.p.' immediately before the typed name of the employee responsible for the letter.

The name of the person signing the letter is typed below the space left for the signature, and is followed on the next line by his position in the company or by the name of the department he represents.

Traditionally the complimentary close and signature have been typed in the middle of the page, but it is becoming more and more common for firms to place them against the left-hand margin.

The example on page 4 does not mention an *enclosure*, nor does it have a *subject line*.

If an enclosure accompanies the letter, this fact is indicated both in the text itself and by the word *Enclosure* (often reduced to *Enc.* or *Encl.*) typed against the left-hand margin some distance below the signature. There are other ways of referring to enclosures—the use of adhesive labels, for instance, or the typing of lines in the left-hand margin beside the reference in the text to the document or documents enclosed—but typing the word *Enclosure* at the bottom of the letter is by far the most common.

The subject matter of a letter is often indicated in a *subject line* which appears below the salutation:

Dear Sirs

<u>Your order no. 6544 of 15 March 1977</u>

The term 'Re-' is seldom used these days to introduce the subject: like other Latin words which have been employed in British correspondence for decades, it is now considered old-fashioned and artificial. (*See Chapter 1*) Subject lines are not always required, and the date of a letter referred to in the first line of the answer is often sufficient to indicate what the subject is.

## STYLE OF AMERICAN FIRMS

Foreign learners of English commercial correspondence should beware of drawing a sharp distinction between British and American styles. The fact of the matter is that the similarities are more striking than the differences, and the differences between British and American English in general are fewer and less important now than they were, say, fifteen or twenty years ago. For correspondence purposes it is quite enough to be familiar with one particular layout and one particular set of conventions, since Americans have no difficulty in understanding British business letters, and *vice versa*. Another point to bear in mind is the fact that the majority of business letters today are written, not by Americans or British people, but by individuals and firms using English as a foreign language. This is another factor which has caused the two styles to merge to a very considerable extent, and provided you follow the advice given in this chapter and elsewhere, your letters will conform to modern business practice.

## TYPES OF BRITISH FIRMS

The *limited liability company*, or *joint stock company*, is the commonest type of firm in the United Kingdom. The company is owned by shareholders, and the term 'limited liability' means that when the full price of a share has been paid the holder has no further liability to contribute money to the company.

The shareholders in a limited company elect a Board of Directors, and these men and women are responsible for looking after the financial interests of those who elect them. The directors appoint one of their number to the position of Managing Director, and he or she is the link between the Board, who make policy decisions, and management, whose function it is to execute the policy determined on. Thus the Managing Director is in charge of the day-to-day running of the company, and in large organisations he is often assisted by a General Manager. The various departmental managers—the Sales Manager, the Personnel

8

Manager, the Chief Buyer, and others—are responsible to the Managing Director for the efficient running of their departments. British company law requires a limited company to have a Company Secretary. (*See Chapter 14*)

Another type of firm is the *partnership*. In this case limited liability does not extend to the whole firm and all partners (even in a *limited partnership* there must be at least one partner with unlimited liability), so partnerships are very seldom manufacturing or trading firms. They tend rather to be professional organisations such as firms of solicitors, auditors, architects, or management consultants. The names of all partners must, in accordance with the law in Britain, be printed on the stationery of a partnership.

## EXERCISES

1. Design a letter heading for a company manufacturing washing machines, refrigerators and other household equipment. Include all the information about your company which is normally shown in a modern letter heading.
2. Write out the following date in three or four different ways in which it might appear at the top of a business letter: *the fourteenth of April nineteen-seventy-eight.*
3. Imagine you are writing to the company whose letter heading appears on page 4. How would you set out the inside address, and what would the salutation and complimentary close be?
4. Below are names and addresses which might appear—suitably set out, of course—in the top left-hand corner of a business letter. Give the correct salutation and complimentary close in each case:
    (*a*) Burke and Sons Ltd., 55 Inkerman Road, London SE5 8BZ.
    (*b*) The Sales Manager, BGW Electrics Ltd., Liverpool 4.
    (*c*) Mr A. L. Moon, British Rail (Southern Region), London W1M 2BT.
    (*d*) Ms Angela Box, Gorton and Sons, 344 Oxford St., London W1A 3BA.
5. Which of the organisations mentioned in Exercise 4 should be addressed as *Messrs.*? Give your reasons for including or omitting *Messrs.* in all four cases.

# 3 | The enquiry

Most letters of enquiry are short and simple, so much so that many firms have adopted the practice of sending printed enquiry forms, thereby eliminating the need for a letter. As a prospective buyer, the writer of an enquiry states briefly and clearly what he is interested in, and this is all the receiver of the letter needs to know.

It is rather different when the object of your enquiry is to obtain a special price for regular orders, or selling rights in your area. In cases like these you are asking for concessions, and you have to 'sell' your proposal to the supplier. This requires much more skill than does the writing of a routine enquiry, and we will be returning to letters of this type shortly.

A first enquiry—a letter sent to a supplier with whom you have not previously done business—should include:

(a) A brief mention of <u>how you obtained your potential supplier's name.</u> Your source may be an embassy, consulate, or chamber of commerce; you may have seen the goods in question at an exhibition or trade fair; you may be writing as the result of a recommendation from a business associate, or on the basis of an advertisement in the daily, weekly or trade press.

(b) Some <u>indication of the demand</u> in your area for the goods which the supplier deals in.

(c) Details of what you would like your prospective supplier to send you. Normally you will be interested in a catalogue, a price list, discounts, methods of payment, delivery times, and, where appropriate, samples.

(d) A <u>closing sentence</u> to round off the enquiry.

Here are some suggestions for sentences which you might include in a routine enquiry:

## Opening lines

1. Your name has been given us by the British Chamber of Commerce in Hamburg, . . .
2. The British Embassy in Copenhagen has advised us to get in touch with you concerning . . .
3. We saw your products demonstrated at the Hanover Fair earlier this year, and would like to know whether . . .
4. Messrs. Rawlingson and Townsend of Bletchley, who we understand have been doing business with you for some years, inform us that you may be able to supply us with . . .
5. We have seen your advertisement in last Sunday's *Observer*, and would be grateful if you would let us have details of . . .
6. Your advertisement in this month's issue of *The Shoemaker* states that you can offer . . .

## Indicating the state of the market

7. There is a brisk demand here for high-quality sports shirts of the type you manufacture.
8. Demand for this type of machine is not high, but sales this year will probably exceed £25,000.
9. These fancy goods are in demand during the tourist season (late May to early September), but for the rest of the year sales are moderate, and often rather low.
10. There is no market here for articles of this type in the higher price ranges, but less expensive models sell very well throughout the year.
11. You can count on a brisk turnover if prices are competitive and deliveries prompt.

## Asking for information

12. Will you please send us your catalogue and price list for . . .
13. Will you please quote prices c.i.f. Amsterdam for the following items in the quantities stated: . . .
14. We would be glad to receive specifications of your new SE11 typewriter, together with your current export price list and details of trade discounts.
15. We are also interested in your terms of payment and in discounts offered for regular purchases and large orders.
16. If we place orders with you we will have to insist on prompt delivery. Can you guarantee delivery within three weeks of receiving orders?
17. We would appreciate a sample of each of the items listed above.

## Closing sentences

18. We are looking forward to hearing from you.
19. We would appreciate a prompt answer.
20. As our own customers are pressing us for a quotation, we hope you will be able to make us an offer within a fortnight from today's date.
21. We hope to hear from you shortly.
22. Since the season will soon be under way, we must ask you to reply by the end of this month.

The first three model letters in this chapter are examples of routine first enquiries. Letters 1 and 2 are addressed direct to suppliers, while no. 3 is written to an agent.

# FOURNIER ET CIE

*Importers of Fashion Goods*                              Avenue Ravigny 14

*PARIS*                                                    Paris XV


JdP/AG                                                    12 October 1978


The Western Shoe Co. Ltd.
Yeovil, Somerset S19 3AF
ENGLAND


Dear Sirs

1  We have heard from the British Embassy in Paris that you are producing for
   export hand-made shoes and gloves in natural materials.

2  There is a steady demand in France for high-quality goods of this type.
   Sales are not high, but a good price can be obtained for fashionable designs.

3  Will you please send us your catalogue and full details of your export prices
   and terms of payment, together with samples of leathers used in your articles
   and, if possible, specimens of some of the articles themselves.

4  We are looking forward to hearing from you.

Yours faithfully        → *the complimentary close*
FOURNIER ET CIE SA


J. Dupont

J. du Pont
Managing Director

# THE JAMESON CONSTRUCTION
### CO. PTY.

*Proprietary = plc in Australia*

Harbour Road

MELBOURNE, AUSTRALIA

HS/ja                                                    25 June 1978

The Aluminium Alloy Co. Ltd.
79 Prince Albert St.
Birmingham B21 8DJ
Great Britain

Dear Sirs

We have seen your advertisement in The Metal Worker, and would be grateful *als u zo vriendelijk*
if you would kindly send us details of your aluminium fittings. *wilt u zij*

Please quote us for the supply of the items listed on the enclosed enquiry
form, giving your prices c.i.f. Melbourne.  Will you please also indicate
delivery times, your terms of payment, and details of discounts for regular
purchases and large orders.

Our annual requirements for metal fittings are considerable, and we (may) be *be bility*
able to place substantial orders with you if your prices are competitive
and your deliveries prompt.

We look forward to receiving your quotation.

Yours faithfully
THE JAMESON CONSTRUCTION CO. PTY.

H. Smithers
Buyer

13

**JAMES SCOTT**

*Photographic Dealer*

DURBAN

J. White & Co.Ltd.
254 Smuts Avenue
Cape Town *South Africa*

5 May 1978

Dear Sirs

I see from the <u>Camera Review</u> that you are the South African agents for
Messrs. Derby and Sons of London.

Would you please send me price lists and catalogues for all DERVIEW products
you stock, as well as details of discounts and terms of payment.  Are you
prepared to grant special terms for annual orders totalling R 35,000 in
value? *Rand*

I would appreciate a visit from your representative when he is next in the
Durban area:  perhaps he could bring some samples of DERVIEW colour
<u>transparencies</u>, which are attracting a good deal of interest here.
*= transparanter, dia's (slides)*
I look forward to your reply.

Yours faithfully

*James Scott*

James Scott

## Notes on letters 1–3

Remember the following combinations of nouns and prepositions:

*demand for*: There is a considerable/a steady/some/little/no demand for
these articles in this area.

*requirements for*: Our requirements for these goods will increase steadily
in the course of the year.

*details of*: Details of your terms of business would be welcomed.

*samples of, specimens of*: We would need samples of materials used, and
specimens of finished articles.

Note these verbs:

*to quote*: Will you please quote us for the following: . . .
Please quote all prices c.i.f. Haugesund.

*to look forward to*: We look forward to meeting your representative.
Our customers are looking forward to *testing* samples of your lines.
The verb *to look forward to* must be followed by a noun or by the form of the relevant verb ending in *-ing*.
*to place*: We will be able to place substantial orders *with* you.

Another very common type of enquiry is one in which a customer asks a supplier for a special product line which the supplier may not already be producing. When writing letters of this type it is essential to explain exactly what is wanted, and in what quantities. A supplier will also need to know whether there are long-term prospects for his article on your market, since otherwise it might not be worth his while manufacturing it. The next model letter is an example of this type of enquiry.

[4] *Enquiry from an import agent in India
to a British export manufacturer*

---

## DYMONT & CO

*General Import Merchants*

---

CALCUTTA

---

Weatherproof Ltd.
Newtown
Liverpool L30 7KE

1 December 1978

Dear Sirs

We have now been importing your "Litewate" raincoats for a number of years, and our trade connections throughout India have been more than satisfied with the garments.

However, two or three Indian manufacturers have recently launched ultra-lightweight models, and these are catching on very fast. In view of the increased competition this involves, we wonder whether you have considered marketing a coat of rather lighter material than the "Litewate", but equally waterproof. A garment of this type would have a large sale in this country if you could offer it at a competitive price, that is to say not more than £3.50 for a man's model, and slightly less for a woman's. You will be interested to learn that raincoats being produced here suffer from one major drawback[2], namely excessive condensation[3] on the inside surface.

We would be grateful for your preliminary comments as soon as possible.

Yours faithfully
DYMONT & CO.

15

Asking a firm with whom you have not done business to supply an urgent order may call for tactful wording, especially in cases such as that mentioned in the next letter.

[5] *Enquiry from an export merchant who has not been able to obtain satisfactory deliveries from his regular suppliers*

# A. ZIMMERLI A.G.

*Import-Export Mechants*     ZURICH

Messrs. W.H. Strong and Co.
73 Crimea Road
London   SE25 3NF
England

23 April 1978

Dear Sirs

We have been given your name by our associates J.J. Mueller of Basle, who inform us that they have been doing business with you for some fifteen years. We asked them if they knew of a manufacturer who might be able to supply at very short notice the articles specified on the enclosed list, and they advised us to contact you.

We can explain in confidence that our normal supplier has rather let us down on delivery dates this year, and we are in danger of getting into arrears with some of our overseas contracts.

If you can supply the goods we require, please accept this as our order.  Payment will be made in accordance with your usual terms of business.

We hope you will be able to help us in this instance, and can add that if your products and terms are as competitive as we have been led to believe, we will be interested in a long-term contract with you.

We would appreciate a reply by telex.

Yours faithfully
A. Zimmerli AG

Bruno Schmidt
Export Manager

Enclosure

# A. B. White & Co. Ltd.
Import and Export

567 Queen Street
London, EC4 8YH

*Directors: A.B. White, T.D. Pearson*

*Telephone:* 494 6130

*JR/ph*

*31 January 1978*

*The Excelso Company Ltd.*
*High Wycombe, Bucks. B84 1WE*

*Dear Sirs*

*We have just received an enquiry from a multi-national organisation owning several luxury hotels in East Africa. They are opening a new hotel next spring, and have asked us to submit quotations for furniture and fittings in accordance with the attached list.*

*The articles in question must be hard-wearing and up-to-date in design, and delivery by February of next year is essential. Will you please let us know, therefore, whether you will be able to complete an order for the quantities required within the time at your disposal.*

*We will also be glad to have an estimate for the number of containers required and the approximate cost of packing.*

*Please let us have your quotation as soon as possible.*

*Yours faithfully*
*A.B. WHITE AND CO. LTD.*

*Jennifer Ring*

*Jennifer Ring (Miss)*
*Overseas Dept.*

## Notes on letters 4–6

The adjective *competitive*, which means *favourably comparable with rival offers*, occurs very frequently in enquiries and letters replying to them, as do the verb *to compete* and the nouns *competition* and *competitor*.

Here are some examples of how these words are used:

Competitive prices and terms are essential if this article is to sell on overseas markets.

These products will have to compete with mass-produced equipment from Asian countries.

Competition in the textile trade has never been keener: our competitors are offering lower prices all the time.

*Explanation of reference numbers in letters 4–6*
[1] *catching on*: Becoming popular or fashionable.
[2] *drawback*: Disadvantage.
[3] *condensation*: Drops of liquid forming, in this case, in tropical climates.
[4] *associates*: People the writer does business with, or people in the same line of business as the writer. *handelspartner*
[5] *let us down*: (in this letter) Failed to execute our orders properly.
[6] *getting into arrears*: Falling behind schedule.
[7] *hard-wearing*: Strong, able to stand up to a lot of use.

Finally, here are some sentences which are commonly used in letters:

*Hinting at future business, requesting special terms, and asking for information about deliveries:*
23. As we do a considerable trade in this line, we expect a keen price.
24. If your goods are up to sample, they should sell readily in this market.
25. If the quality is right and the price competitive, we think we can promise you good results.
26. Provided you can guarantee regular supplies and promise delivery within a fortnight of receiving our orders, we should have no trouble in marketing your products here.
27. As we are the leading dealers in this (town) (area) (country) . . .
28. Since we have connections throughout the country . . .
29. In view of the fact that we are sole agents for this product . . .
30. As our estimated monthly requirements are in the region of 2,000 cases . . .
31. . . . we would like to discuss the possibility of a contract of agency with you.
32. . . . we would like to know whether you would be willing to grant us a special discount.
33. As we are under contract, please let us know whether you can guarantee shipment by 3 July.
34. Would you be able to deliver within 5 weeks of receipt of our order?
35. We require the goods by 1 June at the latest.
36. Please quote your price (f.o.b. Liverpool) (c.i.f. Rio de Janeiro).

*Abbreviations used to indicate to what extent charges for freight, insurance, etc. are included in the price quoted*
*ex-works; ex-factory; ex-mill/mills*: Price without any transport.
\**f.o.r.* (*free on rail*); \**f.o.t.* (*free on truck*): Price includes delivery to the railway and loading on a truck.
\**f.a.s.* (*port named*): Price includes delivery to loading point 'alongside' ship.
\**f.o.b.* (*export port named*): Price includes delivery to docks and loading onto a ship.

18

*f.o.b. (*import port named*) (*particularly used in U.S.A. trade*): Price includes all costs up to arrival in the importing country, but not insurance or unloading.

*c. & f. (*destination named*): Price includes all costs up to the named destination but not insurance.

*c.i.f. (*destination named*): Price includes all costs including insurance, up to named destination.

*ex-ship* (*import port named*): Price includes delivery to the named port of destination; the seller is responsible for the goods until the ship arrives.

*franco quay; ex-dock* (*import port named*): Price includes all costs, unloading, customs duties, etc.

*franco domicilium; free delivered*: Price includes delivery to the premises of the buyer or consignee, customs duties paid by seller or consignor.

The following are used for home trade, in Great Britain:

*carriage paid home*: All transport paid by sender.

*carriage forward*: Transport to be paid by buyer.

*franco; free delivered*: All costs paid by sender.

*C.O.D.*: Goods to be paid for by buyer on delivery.

*cash on delivery.*

## EXERCISES

1. Fill in the missing words:

   We have been _given_ your name _by_ our associates _____ Howard & Co. _of_ Carlisle, who _inform_ us that you have been _____ them with stationery _____ a number of years.

   There is a _great_ demand here _in_ Edinburgh _for_ the qualities you_____, and we believe we could _____ large orders_____ you if your _____ are competitive.

   _____ you please send us your illustrated _____, together with your _____ list and details of your _____ of business.

   We look forward to _____ _____ you.

2. You are J. du Pont, Managing Director of Fournier & Cie SA of Paris. Write to the Western Shoe Co. Ltd., Yeovil, Somerset S19 3AF, England, telling them where you have obtained their name and what you know about them.

   Indicate that there is a good market in France for their products, and then ask them to send you their catalogue and anything else you think you should have. Round off your letter with an encouraging sentence before signing it.

* Capital letters can also be used.

Remember to include the date and inside address, and make sure you use the correct salutation and complimentary close.

When you have finished your letter, compare it with letter no. 1 of this chapter.

3. Use the following notes to compose a letter of enquiry for a firm of importers:

   To the Drake Cycle Company, Wellington, New Zealand: Your new sports models seen at the Birmingham Trade Fair. Request details all models, catalogue, price list, terms, delivery times. Requirements: 50 each, women's and men's. Discounts? Future supply position?

4. Write a letter of enquiry on behalf of your firm to the Yorkshire Woollen Company, Bradford, asking for patterns of cloth for men's suits.

5. Write to the import agent for RITESWIFT typewriters, enquiring about prices, delivery dates, and any other facts which you, as a prospective customer, would be interested in.

6. Your firm is a Swiss manufacturing company and is in urgent need of certain metal fittings which cannot be obtained quickly enough from the normal suppliers. Write an enquiry to a British maker of these fittings.

7. You have seen an advertisement in the trade press for a small electric motor made in England. Write to the manufacturer, asking for full details and offering your services as an import agent.

8. Write to your buying agent in another country, enclosing a list of luxury goods you need before Christmas. Prompt delivery is of the utmost importance in this case.

# 4 | Replies to enquiries: offers

A reply to an enquiry from a regular customer is normally fairly brief, and does not need to be more than polite and direct. Provided the supplier is in a position to meet his correspondent's requirements, his reply will generally:

(a) Thank the writer of the letter of enquiry for the letter in question.

(b) Supply all the information requested, and refer both to enclosures and to samples, catalogues and other items being sent by separate post.

(c) Provide additional information, not specifically requested by the customer, so long as it is relevant.

(d) Conclude with one or two lines encouraging the customer to place orders and assuring him of good service.

Replies to enquiries may begin in a number of ways. Here are some suggestions:

*Opening lines*

1. Many thanks for your enquiry of 3 April . . .
2. We are pleased to have your enquiry about . . .
3. We thank you for your letter of 6 January, in which you enquire about . . .
4. In reply to your telex of today . . .
5. Replying to your enquiry of 2 June . . .
6. . . . we are pleased to inform you that . . .
7. . . . we have pleasure in confirming that we can . . .
8. . . . we can offer you immediately . . .
9. We thank you for your enquiry, and are pleased to inform you that our Brazilian agents hold stocks of all our products.
10. In reply to your enquiry of 8 August we are enclosing . . .
11. . . . the brochures you requested.
12. . . . full particulars of our export models.
13. . . . our revised price list.
14. We thank you for your letter of 4 July and have sent you today, by separate post, . . .
15. . . . samples of all our wax polishes.
16. . . . patterns of our new silk fabrics.
17. . . . specimens of our latest ball-point pens.
18. . . . a full range of samples.

As an illustration, here is an answer to letter no. 1, page 12:

# Western Shoe Company Ltd.

YEOVIL, SOMERSET S19 3AF

ENGLAND

SG/EO                                                      15 October 1978

Fournier et Cie SA
Avenue Ravigny 14
Paris XV
France

Dear Sirs

We thank you for your enquiry of 12 October, and appreciate your interest
in our products.

Details of our export prices and terms of payment are enclosed, and we have
arranged for a copy of our catalogue to be sent to you today.

Our representative for Europe, Mr J.Needham, will be in Paris from the
24th to the 30th of this month, and we have asked him to make an
appointment to visit you during this period.  He will have with him a
full range of samples of our hand-made lines, and is authorised to
discuss the terms of an order with you or to negotiate a contract.
to discuss ath → direct object
We think our articles will be just what you want for the fashionable
trade, and look forward to the opportunity of doing business with you.

Yours faithfully
WESTERN SHOE COMPANY LTD.

S. Granville
Export Sales Manager

22

As further examples of letters of a 'routine' character, here are suggested replies to letters 2 and 3, Chapter 3:

[1] *Reply to letter no. 2, page 13*

 **Aluminium Alloy Co. Ltd.   Birmingham**

79 Prince Albert St.    Birmingham B21 8DJ    Great Britain

The Jameson Construction Co. Pty.                    2 July 1978
Harbour Road
Melbourne 6
Australia

Dear Sirs        *to list items*

We thank you for your letter of 25 June, and are glad to inform you that all
the items listed in your enquiry are in stock.  We are enclosing a pro-
forma invoice for the aluminium fittings you are interested in:  if you
wish to place a firm order, will you please arrange for settlement of the
invoice by draft through your bank, and advise us at the same time.

We can guarantee delivery in Melbourne within 3 weeks of receiving your
instructions.  If you require the items urgently, we will arrange for them
to be sent by air, but this will, of course, entail higher freight charges.

We are enclosing details of our terms of payment, and would be happy to
discuss discounts with you if you would kindly let us know how large your
orders are likely to be.

We are also enclosing a copy of the report, which appeared in the March
issue of The Metal Worker, on our ALUMOY fittings.

We are looking forward to hearing from you, and assure you that your
orders will receive our immediate attention.

Yours faithfully

*[signature]*

# J. WHITE & CO. LTD.

*Photographic Supplies*                                    CAPE TOWN

7 May 1978

James Scott
Photographic Dealer
Durban

Dear Mr Scott

Many thanks for your letter of 5 May. We are interested to hear
that you saw our advertisement in the Camera Review, and appreciate
your interest in the DERVIEW products we stock.

We are enclosing our Terms of Business, where you will find details
of our quarterly discounts, and our price list for the complete
range of DERVIEW products. As you will see, we can grant special
terms for orders of the value you mention.

I will be in Durban myself on 17 May, and will be happy to call on
you at any time in the afternoon. Perhaps you would like to let
me know whether this is convenient. I will, of course, bring the
complete range of DERVIEW colour transparencies, which are
described in the catalogue we have sent you today.

I am looking forward to meeting you.

Yours faithfully

*Dick Richards*

[3] *Suggested reply to letter no. 6, page 17 which was an enquiry made through a buying agent*

---

**The Excelso Company Ltd.**
*Specialists in Modern Design*                    Directors: J. Corner, B. Edge

High Wycombe, Bucks.
Telephone: 0494 6130


Our Ref:H/f150 Your Ref:JR/ph                    3 February 1978


Attention Miss Jennifer Ring, Overseas Dept.
A.B. White & Co. Ltd.
567 Queen Street
London EC4 8YH


Dear Sirs

We thank you for your enquiry of 31 January, and can confirm
our telephone conversation of yesterday, in which we informed
you that we can deliver part of the goods required from stock,
in accordance with the enclosed detailed offer.   For the
balance we would require approximately three weeks from the
date of receiving your confirmation that this arrangement is
acceptable.

Prices as quoted are f.o.b. London.
Packing in wooden cases.
Delivery as specified above.
Payment against documents, by banker's draft.

We hope your client will find our terms and delivery dates
satisfactory, and we can assure you that you may count on
our full co-operation and attention in this matter.


Yours faithfully

*Simon Davies*

---

Letters 1, 2 and 3 are examples of answers to enquiries of a routine character, and they are written in plain, direct English. They give the information asked for, and this is basically all that is wanted.

Let us consider next the firm which is keen to increase sales, or one which is putting a new product on the market. A great deal of time, know-how and money has probably been spent on promoting the product

25

or products concerned, and the task of actually selling the goods begins with answering the enquiries as they come in.

The letter of reply must now fulfil the function of a salesman: it must contain information which will sustain the reader's interest and persuade him or her to place an order. In such cases the style of the letter is of great importance.

The letter must be convincing: it must create enthusiasm by the freshness and originality of its approach, and this cannot be done by using routine phrases.

The letter which follows is a reply to letter no. 4, Chapter 3, page 15. The enquirer was already very interested in the manufacturer's goods, so the manufacturer has only to give the information asked for. Notice, however, how he shows interest in his prospective customer's special needs.

[4] *more to promote the products, rather than an answer to an enquiry*

Dear Sirs

We are very glad to have your letter of 1 December and to hear that you have been receiving enquiries about our *Weatherproof* coats.

The *Litewate* range you mention has been a great success wherever it has been introduced, and we are already exporting it to several tropical countries, in both Asia and Africa. Unlike many waterproof coats, the *Litewate* does not cause excessive condensation on the inside surface, and so would be suitable for your climate. *buitensporig*

We can quote you the following prices:

|  |  |  |  | £ | p |
|---|---|---|---|---|---|
| 250 *Litewate* coats, women's, | | medium | | 375 | 00 |
| 250 | ,, | ,, | ,, small | 375 | 00 |
| 250 | ,, | ,, men's, | medium | 493 | 75 |
| 250 | ,, | ,, | ,, small | 431 | 25 |
| | | F.O.B. Liverpool | | 1,675 | 00 |
| Freight Liverpool–Calcutta | | | | 50 | 20 |
| Insurance | | | | 18 | 30 |
| | | | | 1,743 | 50 |

We will be able to ship the raincoats within 2–3 weeks of receiving your order.

We are grateful to you for your suggestion concerning an ultra-lightweight coat for the Indian market, and are pleased to inform you that we have been looking into the question of a suitable material for some time now. Our Research Department assure us that they will have a model ready in the very near future, and we will come back to the matter as soon as we have some definite news for you. *been raak onderzoeken*

We are enclosing full details of our terms of business, and have sent you by separate post a set of descriptive brochures of our products, and a supply of sales literature.

We look forward to hearing from you again.

Yours faithfully

*to ensure : de garantie geven*
*assure : de verzekering ,,*

Letters 5 and 6 are further examples of the modern method, and like letter no. 4 they show that there is room for individuality in modern commercial correspondence.

[5] *From a manufacturer to a large retailer*

---

# MODERN PLASTICS LTD.
Manufacturers of Plasticware

Melox House
PORTSMOUTH

RBG/hk

12 January 1978

Messrs. L. Thoms & Son
150 Beachview Avenue
Bournemouth H77 6OP

Dear Sirs

We are very pleased to have your enquiry, and are enclosing the price-list you requested, together with our terms of sale.

As you have evidently realized, plastic kitchenware is here to stay - it has already ousted heavy and expendable metal, glass and china from the modern kitchen.  Dealers who have displayed our brightly coloured range have reported good sales even in the present season, when hardware sales are usually at their lowest.

After studying our prices and our liberal terms to the trade, you will understand why we are working to capacity to meet the demand.  We would advise you, therefore, to let us have your order by the end of the month, as this will enable you to have stocks of our attractive lines by Easter.

We look forward to the opportunity of being of service to you.

Yours faithfully
p.p. MODERN PLASTICS LTD.

*R. B. Gordon*

R. B. Gordon
Sales Manager

---

Why is this a good letter?

Discuss this question with your fellow-students. Then compare your views with the suggestions given after the exercises at the end of this chapter.

## [6]

Dear Sirs

In your letter of 1 May you ask us to send you samples of our rubberised floor coverings for use on rough surfaces. We appreciate your interest, and have today despatched a range of qualities which we have selected specially to meet your needs.

All of these materials are robust and hard-wearing, and we particularly recommend no. 7—COMPO—which is a synthetic substance developed by our research department to withstand the wear and tear of rough and uneven floors.

Please give the samples any test you wish: we are confident that they will stand up to the roughest handling.

Our price-list is enclosed with this letter, together with our trade terms, as we think you will need these when you have completed your tests. It will be a pleasure to quote you terms for contract supplies, and our technical representatives are at your service at all times.

Yours faithfully

A request for a special discount may call for some thought, and a counter-proposal may be made in reply, as in letter no. 7.

## [7]

Dear Sirs

Many thanks for your letter of 15 July, in which you ask us for an extra discount of 2½% over and above the usual trade discounts in connection with your order for 30,000 envelopes no. 2M.

While we appreciate your order, we feel we must point out that our prices have already been cut to the minimum possible, and that envelopes are unobtainable elsewhere at these rates.

However, we would be willing to allow you a special 2½% discount if you could see your way to increasing your order to 50,000.

We await your reply.

Yours faithfully

## OFFERS OF GOODS AND SERVICES

In many types of business it is the practice of the seller to offer goods to his regular customers and to others who may be interested, without waiting for an enquiry. Similarly, suppliers regularly make special offers of goods when prices are particularly favourable. In these cases the customer's interest has to be aroused.

28

## [8] *Offer of Brazilian coffee*

Dear Sirs

You will be interested to hear that we have been able to obtain a further supply of Brazilian coffee of the same quality as that we supplied you with last year. The total consignment is only 10,000 kg., and we are pleased to offer it to you at 60p per kg. With the increases in freight charges which become effective next month, the next consignment will be rather dearer, so we recommend you to take advantage of this offer, which is firm for five days only, and to telex your order without delay.

Yours faithfully

## [9] *French wine exporter's offer to British importer*

Dear Sirs

Messrs. Hankinson and Co. of Towgate St., with whom we have been doing business for a number of years, have informed us that you will probably be replenishing your stocks of French white wines in the near future.

You will already know that we had an exceptionally good season in 1973, and that the fine quality of our white vintages of that year is renowned both in your country and in ours.

We are now shipping these wines, and would be very glad to welcome you as customers. Our full export price-list is enclosed, but we would like to draw your attention particularly to our

White Bordeaux      @    £60.00 per gross bottles, and
Sauterne            @    £70.00  ,,      ,,       ,,

These wines have always sold very well in Britain, and the prices quoted above for bulk purchase will enable you to sell at highly competitive prices, while obtaining a good margin of profit.

We will be pleased to supply you with a first order against settlement within 30 days of date of invoice, and with $2\frac{1}{2}\%$ discount. Immediate shipment from Bordeaux is guaranteed.

We advise you to place your order promptly, since we expect considerable response from other foreign customers to this special offer.

Yours faithfully

## [10] *Fruit broker's offer to wholesaler*

Dear Sirs

Confirming our telephone conversation of this morning, we are pleased to be able to offer you the following South African fruit, which arrived yesterday with the S.S. *Durham Castle*:

| | |
|---|---|
| 300 boxes 'Early Rivers' plums | £0.55 per box |
| 100 boxes 'Golden Glory' peaches | £1.10 per box |
| 200 boxes 'Prime Yellow' apricots | £0.50 per box. |

These brands are well known to you, and the consignment in question is well up to the high quality of previous years. The fruit is excellently packed and would reach you in perfect condition.

We would be glad to send the goods by rail on receipt of your order, which should be sent by telephone or telex. The price includes carriage, and is firm for 24 hours only.

Yours faithfully

**[11]** *Battery manufacturer's offer to overseas dealer*

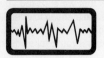

# NIPPONEX ELECTRICS

### TOKYO, JAPAN

Amperlite Ltd.
146 O'Leary St.
Dublin 2
Ireland                                              27 December 1978

Dear Sirs

DRILITE BATTERIES

Improved methods of production enable us to offer you our range of <u>Drilite</u>
batteries at a reduced price for large quantities.

Details of the new prices for your market are enclosed, and you will see that
the average price reduction is 5%. As our prices are quoted c.i.f. Dublin,
you will agree that they are considerably lower than those of manufacturers
of similar batteries, both here in Japan and elsewhere.

The quality of our products remains the same - only the finest chemicals are
used.    The new prices are for minimum orders of £1,000 and are effective
as from 1 January.    Immediate despatch is guaranteed, and we hold ample
stocks.

We appreciate your past custom, and look forward to supplying you in the
new year at the new prices.

Yours faithfully
NIPPONEX ELECTRICS


Enclosure

---

Letters 12, 13 and 14 are examples of letters making special offers of
goods at reduced prices.

**[12]** *Circular from a large store informing customers of sale of stocks
at reduced prices*

Dear Sir or Madam

On 1 June this year we are moving to larger and more modern premises at nos. 50–55
Oxford Street. Our business has grown so considerably in recent years that we can no

30

longer provide our customers with the service we are used to giving them in our present building.

In view of this move we are selling off our entire stock at greatly reduced prices to save us the trouble and expense of packing and removal.

Come and visit us any day next week. The sale will last for *7 days only*—less if stocks are cleared sooner. This is an exceptional opportunity for you to obtain real bargains: reductions range from 15% to 30%, while certain surplus lines will be going at up to 50% off list prices.

Don't miss this chance! Our doors open at 9 a.m. on Monday 20 May.

## [13] *Offer of special trade discount*

Dear Sirs

In last summer's exceptionally fine weather we were so overloaded with late orders from most of our regular customers that we were unable to keep pace with the demand. While we understand our customers' fear of overstocking, we are sure they will appreci- ate our position when we are suddenly flooded with urgent last-minute orders.

To encourage all customers to lay in a good opening stock this year, we are prepared to offer a special trade discount of 4% on all orders over £500 net value received before the end of the month.

Help us by helping yourselves!

Yours faithfully

## [14] *Wholesaler's special offer of woollen blankets*

Dear Sirs

A few weeks ago we were fortunate enough to have the offer of the entire stock of the Hartley Blanket Company, which has now ceased to manufacture woollen products. We took advantage of this exceptional opportunity, and are now in a position to offer these famous all-wool blankets well below the market price.

This is a 'once-in-a-lifetime' opportunity, and we expect to clear our stock in a few days. We must ask you, therefore, to give the enclosed special price list your immediate attention and to let us have your order at once.

Orders will be executed in strict rotation and can only be accepted as long as stocks last.

Yours faithfully

It often happens that after answering an enquiry, a firm receives no further news from its prospective customer. Very few customers write and tell those who send them quotations why they do not wish to place an order. The practice of sending a representative to call on the enquirer soon after the enquiry is answered is common, as is that of sending a follow-up letter. Letter no. 15 is a specimen of a follow-up letter to a distributor to whom a catalogue was sent in response to his enquiry.

## [15]

Dear Mr Morton

You wish to modernise your store-rooms with the most up-to-date shelving system yet devised: that is clear because you asked for our catalogue, which was sent to you earlier this month.

31

The next step lies, of course, with you. You could have a demonstration of the fitting of the LOCKSHELF system in your own store-room, or see the combined units here in our showrooms.

You could test for yourself the wonderful <u>adaptability</u> of our system to all storage problems, by sending us a trial order for one 5 metre section, which <u>comprises</u> three units. Or if you have any special problems, you are welcome to our advice without any obligation.

You may be sure that whichever of our services you decide to use, you will receive our immediate attention.

Yours sincerely

Here is a selection of phrases for use in making offers and quotations:

## Opening lines

19. We have pleasure in . . .
20. . . . quoting as follows for . . .
21. . . . submitting the following quotation . . .
22. . . . offering you the following goods . . .
23. . . . enclosing our estimate for the supply of . . .
24. . . . sending you our latest catalogue . . .
25. You will be interested (in) (to hear that) . . .
26. You will find enclosed with this letter a sample of . . .
27. We are pleased to inform you . . .
28. As a result of the favourable supply situation we are able to offer you firm, for immediate delivery . . .

## Prices and terms

29. Our prices are quoted . . .
30. . . . f.o.b. Liverpool/f.a.s. Liverpool.
31. . . . c.i.f. Hamburg/c.i.f. London.
32. Our prices include packing and carriage.
33. Freight and packing cases are included in the price.
34. The price quoted includes packing in special export cases.
35. Price includes delivery to nearest railhead.
36. All prices are ex-works . . .
37. Our (quotations) (prices) are subject to $2\frac{1}{2}$% discount for cash.
38. Prices are subject to variation without notice, in accordance with market fluctuations.
39. The prices quoted are net.
40. Our catalogue prices are less 25% to bona-fide dealers.
41. For quantities of 1 gross and over, we can offer a discount of $12\frac{1}{2}$% on list prices.
42. We can quote you (£2.50 per litre) (£1.15 per dozen) (£1.65 per metre) (£1.75 per sq. metre) (£3.50 per 5 litre drum).
43. Prices for the quality you mention range from 75p to £5.
44. Prices have (risen) (fallen) (remained steady).
45. Raw material prices have risen.
46. Owing to the slump in commodity prices we can offer you these goods . . .
47. . . . at below market price.
48. . . . at less than cost.
49. . . . at the very special price of . . .
50. . . . on very favourable terms.

51. ... at cost price.
52. Our terms are (net cash) (spot cash) (cash within 7 days) (cash on delivery) (cash with order).
53. Our terms are payment on invoice.
54. Our terms are (monthly) (quarterly) settlement.
55. Our terms are 33⅓% discount to approved accounts, with 2½% for settlement within 15 days of date of invoice.
56. Our terms and conditions of sale as printed on our invoices must be strictly observed.
57. Our terms of payment are settlement by last day of month of receipt of our statement.
58. Payment by (banker's draft) (irrevocable letter of credit) (bill of exchange) is requested. *(See also Banking, Chapter 9)*
59. Payment for an initial order would be required on pro-forma invoice.
60. We should require payment by banker's draft on acceptance of your order.

## Conditions and qualifications

61. This offer is (firm for 3 days) (subject to contract).
62. We offer these goods subject to their being unsold on receipt of your order.
63. This offer must be withdrawn if not accepted within 7 days.
64. This is a special offer and is not subject to our usual discounts.
65. Please let us have your order by 31 January, as this price concession will not apply after that date.
66. Goods ordered from our old catalogue can be supplied only until stocks are exhausted.
67. This is a special offer and cannot be repeated.
68. Please note that goods supplied on approval must be returned, carriage paid, within 7 days if not required.

## Supply and demand

69. In view of the heavy demand for this line, we advise you to order at once.
70. The exceptional demand this season has nearly cleared our stocks of . . .
71. This article is in great demand.
72. Owing to the increased demand for this type of car, our stocks have run very low.
73. There is no demand here for such goods.
74. Tropical fruit is in good supply just now.
75. We shall be unable to obtain further supplies.
76. We should be pleased to supply you on a consignment basis.
77. As we have a good supply of these machines we can effect shipment within 5 days.
78. The model you ask for is out of production, but we can supply . . . instead.
79. We can offer you a wide (range) (choice) (selection) of sizes and types from stock.
80. These goods are available immediately from stock.
81. We advise you to stock up while supplies are available.
82. We cannot promise delivery before 1st January unless your order reaches us within 7 days.
83. These shirts can now be had in assorted colours and sizes.
84. Our comprehensive stocks enable us to execute all orders promptly and to our customers' specifications.
85. Supplies of this commodity on world markets greatly exceed the demand.

## Asking for instructions

86. Will you kindly let us have an early decision.
87. Please send us your instructions by (cable) (telex).

88. Please (wire) (cable) (telephone) your order.
89. Kindly confirm your order at the price quoted.
90. We await your instructions by return.
91. If you accept our quotation, please advise us by telex.
92. Your reply by return would be appreciated.
93. Please let us know your wishes by (Friday next) (Friday without fail).
94. Please quote Catalogue no. and colour required when you order.
95. If you let us have your instructions by midday Thursday at the latest we could ship your order by *S.S. Orion*, which sails on 23 August.
96. Kindly use the enclosed order form when you make out your order as this will facilitate prompt and accurate execution.
97. If our proposal is acceptable to you, please confirm by return.

## Concluding sentences

98. Our whole experience is at your service. We hope you will make use of it.
99. We think we have covered every point of your enquiry. If not, please do not hesitate to write to us again. It will be a pleasure to give you an immediate reply.
100. We should appreciate the opportunity of showing you how efficiently we can serve you.
101. Words alone will not prove what we claim for our products: only a trial can do that, and a trial will convince you.
102. The enclosed catalogue will give you all the essential facts about our lines, but it cannot answer all your personal questions. It will be a pleasure for us to do that if you will write to us.
103. You may rely on us to give your requirements immediate attention.
104. We are sure that these goods will meet your requirements, and we look forward to your first order.
105. We will hold a quantity in reserve for you, as we feel sure you would not wish to miss such an opportunity.
106. We look forward to the pleasure of serving you.
107. An early reply would help us to help you.
108. If you think our offer meets your requirements, please let us have your order at an early date, as supplies are limited.
109. As we execute all orders in strict rotation, we strongly advise you to order early.
110. Our services are at your disposal.

## Some vocabulary of Chapter 4

*adaptability*: Ability to be used for more than one purpose; (*adj.*) adaptable; (*v.*) adapt.

*balance* (*n.*): Remainder.

*bargain* (*n.*): Something obtained at a price below its value; (*v.*) bargain = negotiate a price.

*become effective*: Begin to operate.

*bulk purchase*: Buying in large quantities.

*call on*: To visit.

*consignment*: Goods packed together and sent from seller to buyer.

*condensation*: Drops of liquid forming, due to heat, etc.

*contract supplies*: Large quantities ordered under contract.

*demand* (*n.*): Number of orders.

*discount*: Reduction in price allowed by the seller.

*draft*: An order for payment, drawn up by a bank.

*entail*: To cause, involve.

*evidently*: Clearly, obviously.

*excessive*: Too much.

*expendable*: Short lived, not durable.

*the fashionable trade*: Business in high quality clothes.

*firm for five days*: Open for five days.

*firm order*: Definite order.

*grant (v.)*: To allow.

*if stocks are cleared*: If all goods are sold.

*if you could see your way to increasing*: If you agree to increase.

*in stock*: Available, ready for delivery.

*in strict rotation*: In the very same order in which they arrive.

*keep pace with*: Produce fast enough to meet.

*knowhow*: Specialised knowledge, expertise.

*liberal*: Generous.

*lines*: Products or groups of products.

*negotiate*: Discuss (terms, conditions).

*ousted*: Taken the place of.

*overstocking*: Ordering more than can be sold.

*premises*: Buildings or offices where a business is carried on.

*pro-forma invoice*: Invoice enabling a customer to see how much a consignment will cost.

*promote a product*: Make the public aware of a product.

*prospective*: Potential.

*range*: Selection of different products.

*replenish*: Replace what has been consumed.

*robust*: Strong.

*sales literature*: Advertising material.

*settlement*: Payment.

*sustain*: To keep up, maintain.

*trade terms*: Prices paid by the dealer.

*transparencies*: Pictures projected onto a screen.

*ultra-lightweight*: Very light indeed.

*vintages*: Wines from grapes of particular years.

*well up to*: At least as good as.

*without any obligation*: Free from any need to buy.

*withstand*: Resist.

*working to capacity*: Fully occupied.

## EXERCISES

1. Fill in the missing words:

   Thank you _____ your _____ _____ 16 November, _____ which you enquire _____ toys imported _____ Hong Kong. We are _____ to hear that there is a _____ for goods _____ this type _____ Northern Ireland.

   We are _____ our price list and terms of _____, and our catalogue has already been _____ _____ separate post.

   As you will notice, our prices are extremely _____, and since we hold large _____ of all models _____ all times, we can promise delivery _____ a week _____ receipt _____ orders.

   We hope to _____ from you soon, and _____ forward _____ _____ business _____ you.

2. An enquiry has come to your company, a firm of watchmakers, from a British retailer. Write a reply to send with your price-list. Quote your terms, and add any information you consider might induce your correspondent to place orders with you.

3. Answer a foreign letter of enquiry which your firm has received following an exhibition of your sewing machines at a trade fair in Brussels.

4. Write a reply to letter no. 5, Chapter 3, page 16.

5. Compose a letter for your firm, who are producers of tinned food products, to an importer overseas. Offer your standard lines and one new product.

6. Your company is a textile importer. Write a circular letter offering your wholesale customers your old season's stock at reduced prices, and explaining why you are able to do so.

7. Write an answer to the enquiry in sentence no. 14, Chapter 3, page 11.

*Suggested answers to the question on letter 5 on page 27*
It is friendly and direct in style.
It is confident and positive.
It presents the case from the buyer's point of view: there is more 'you' than 'we' in it.
It stimulates interest by quoting successful sales elsewhere, and gives a reason for placing an immediate order.
And finally, it reads like a personal message—not a mass-produced, routine reply.

# 5 | Orders and execution of orders

If the seller's offer is right, an order may be expected to follow. The really difficult part of the business is now over and the remaining correspondence is largely routine. The supplier must, however, maintain the friendly, helpful attitude of his earlier letters in all later correspondence. At all stages of a transaction he must show the buyer that his aim is to serve him well. Difficulties may arise at any time: unforeseen problems may occur and misunderstandings ensue. All these things will need action and explanation, so that careful wording may be required in a letter to keep a customer in the right frame of mind. In other words, every letter written to him should be a 'silent salesman' and a lasting advertisement for the writer. It is only in formal letters of advice and instruction that a correspondent should rely on formal phraseology.

The buyer is able to write without such careful choice of language and is therefore brief and 'to the point', but the modern tendency towards an easier and more natural style in writing is also noticeable here: courtesy costs nothing and a friendly attitude often wins a similar response, all of which can only help trade and improve business relations.

In this chapter, we are dealing largely with the export order, so that one or two routine matters should be dealt with before we turn to the wording of communications.

First of all, accuracy is essential in the placing of an order. An error in quoting a catalogue number, or a mistyped figure in the quantity column can cause trouble which it may be impossible to put right later. All this is very elementary, but such errors are known to occur; a double check at all stages is the only prudent course.

Clarity is also essential. The buyer must make clear to the seller exactly what he wants. Most firms will agree that there is room for improvement here. In the export business there are also other things needed besides an accurate description of the goods: for example, method of transport, packing, delivery and insurance, or possibly method of payment, if this has not been settled already. Then the buyer may require some special documents for his own use or to satisfy import regulations. These must be asked for—the exporter cannot always know what the buyer requires in this respect. Large firms will most probably use an export order form for ordering; the special requirements are printed on this form, and possibly also details of terms and conditions of purchase. A specimen of one of these is given on page 38.

When ordering goods, a customer will generally include the following in his letter:

(a) A reference to a visit by the supplier's representative, or to an advertisement or catalogue, or to a sample, or to previous correspondence. This applies particularly to a *first* order. In subsequent orders the buyer may begin his letter with:

(b) Details of the goods required: quantity, quality, catalogue number, packing, etc.

(c) Conditions and qualifications.

(d) Alternatives which are acceptable if the goods ordered are not available.

(e) A closing sentence, perhaps encouraging the supplier to execute the order promptly and with care.

The following letter illustrates the points listed above:

# FOURNIER ET CIE

*Importers of Fashion Goods*

*PARIS*

Avenue Ravigny 14

Paris XV

The Western Shoe Co. Ltd.
Yeovil, Somerset S19 3AF
England

30 October 1978

Dear Sirs

*a.* Thank you for your letter of 15 October.  As you will already know,
your Mr J. Needham called on us a few days ago and left a range of
samples.  We think articles of this quality will find a ready
market here, and we are prepared to order the following as a
<u>stock trial order:</u> *gewone proe/bestelling*

*b.* 20  "Angela" evening bags,        catalogue no. 5
    50  "Veronica" beauty boxes,      catalogue no. 17
    50  "Daphne" handbags,            catalogue no. 27a
    50  "Gloria" handbags,            catalogue no. 28

*c.* If nos. 27a and 28 are not available for immediate delivery, as
Mr Needham suggested might be the case, please send nos. 27 and
28a instead.

Since we must have the goods on display in time for the Christmas
season, our order is placed on condition that they are despatched
by 10 November at the latest.

As soon as we receive your confirmation and pro-forma invoice,
we will arrange for settlement by banker's transfer.

We are looking forward to hearing from you shortly.

Yours faithfully

FOURNIER ET CIE SA

Here is a list of expressions regularly used when ordering goods:

## *Opening phrases*

1. Thank you for your offer of 1 July, which we accept on the terms quoted.
2. Many thanks for your quotation for stationery. Please send us at once:
3. Thank you for your catalogue and price list. Kindly send us as soon as possible:
4. We enclose our order no. 47791 for . . .
5. Our indent no. B 46215 is enclosed.
6. We have pleasure in ordering the following articles from your winter catalogue:
7. Thank you for letting us have samples of . . . We would be glad if you would supply us with . . .
8. Will you please arrange immediate despatch of:
9. Please send through our forwarding agents, K. Jones and Co. Ltd., Sunderland Avenue, Southampton, the following goods:

## *Referring to quality, etc.*

10. The quality must be up to sample . . .
11. Weight and colour must be as sample supplied . . .
12. First-class material and workmanship are essential.
13. A medium quality would be suitable . . .
14. Only fruit packed so as to be in fresh condition on arrival can be accepted.
15. Please send only pure wool. Mixtures are unsuitable.
16. We must point out that the machines must be guaranteed to be to our own specification.
17. The material must match the enclosed pattern.
18. Please supply in assorted colours, preferably 6 dozen each of red, yellow, green, blue and brown.
19. There is no market here for the higher-priced cameras. Please send only models in the medium price-range.
20. All grades of cotton (jute, tea, fibre, etc.) are acceptable, but we prefer top qualities.
21. The alcohol content must not be under 15%.
22. We enclose a trial order. If the quality is up to our expectations, we shall send further orders in the near future.
23. The material supplied must be absolutely waterproof and we place our order subject to this guarantee.
24. We are arranging for the consignment to be inspected before shipment and must ask you to send only goods in perfect condition.
25. Send us also approx. 1 gross 'seconds'; provided that these are not scratched, we can sell them.
26. All lengths supplied must be cut to the exact dimensions quoted in your offer.
27. Marks or blemishes on the surface may make it necessary for us to reject the goods.
28. A superior finish is important: a rough appearance would be quite unacceptable.
29. The bodywork must have a matt finish inside and a high-gloss exterior.
30. The minimum quantity required is 500 kg. but we would accept up to a maximum of 800 kg. if the quality is high.
31. The over-all length must not exceed 2 metres, and the total weight must not be above 25 kg.

## *Alternative goods*

32. If pattern no. 63A is not available please send 64, 65 or 66A instead.
33. Please supply the nearest you have to the enclosed sample.

- 34. As we are out of this line, please send the nearest you have in stock.
- 35. We leave it to your discretion to supply a suitable substitute, should you not have what we want, but the price must not exceed £1.75 per kg.
- 36. If you have a similar article but of better quality, please supply it instead, provided the price is not more than 10% higher.
- 37. We are prepared to pay up to £8.75, but only for a first-class article. Please send us details of other makes, if you cannot supply at or below this price.
- 38. Please supply in no. 3 Ivory or no. 4 Cream finish if these articles are not available in no. 2 White, as shipment must be effected by S.S. *Diogenes*, sailing on 3 May.

## *Invoicing, Packing, Shipping, Payment*
See special chapters

## *Rejecting an offer*
- 39. Many thanks for your offer of 3 March. We are sorry to have to tell you that we cannot make use of it at present.
- 40. We thank you for your offer and will bear it in mind, should we have need of such equipment at any time.
- 41. Thank you for your quotation for the supply of . . . but we have been obliged to place our order elsewhere in this instance.
- 42. Many thanks for your reply to our enquiry for steel furniture. We will keep your catalogue for further reference, but think your products too highly priced for this market.
- 43. We appreciate your offer of a reduced price, but are of the opinion that the market would not stand an article of this quality at all.

## *Cancellation, Warning of cancellation*
- 44. Our indent is enclosed, but we must ask you to cancel any items which you cannot execute by 1 January.
- 45. Please delete from the order any goods which you (cannot supply ex-stock) (cannot ship within 14 days) (cannot supply exactly to sample).
- 46. We must insist on the observance of our terms and conditions. If you cannot do this, we regret that we shall have to cancel the order.
- 47. Please supply such items as you have in stock, but treat all others as cancelled. Your immediate advice would be appreciated.
- 48. As you have failed to deliver within the specified time, we have no alternative but to cancel our order.
- 49. The recent slump in the market here makes it unavoidable for us to cancel the remainder of our order.
- 50. We regret having to cancel our order for the two further machines, but the worsening of the trading position here gives us no option.
- 51. Please cancel our order no. 33 of 3 October for 25 battery-operated sets and send us all-mains sets in substitution.

## *Prices, Discounts, etc.*
See also Chapter 7
- 52. We agree to your price, but should like to know if you are prepared to grant us a discount of 5% for a quantity of 2,000.
- 53. What special discount can you offer for orders over £5,000 net?
- 54. We enclose our order, but must point out that the falling market here will leave us little or no margin of profit. We must ask you for a keener price in respect of future supplies.

55. As we have now done business with you for a year, we should appreciate quarterly settlement terms.
56. As we propose to run a series of 12 consecutive advertisements, we should like to know what discount you can allow for this.
57. We attach our order for 3 gross, but could send you much larger orders if you could see your way to bringing your price down to a level comparable with that of your competitors in this market.

## Concluding lines

58. Your early attention to this order will be appreciated.
59. Please note that delivery is required by 5 April without fail.
60. If this first order is satisfactorily executed we shall place further business with you.
61. We will do our best with these goods, and if sales are satisfactory we shall make your brand one of our standard lines. Kindly advise us when the goods are despatched.

Most of the model letters which follow in this chapter are adaptable to home or foreign trade, although some are shown in the form of correspondence between British firms.

Now here are a few more letters from buyers to sellers:

## [1] *Importer's order for bell-wire*

Dear Sirs

Many thanks for your prompt reply of 20 April to our enquiry for bell-wire. We enclose our official order for 15,000 metres, which we understand you can supply from stock.

As we pointed out in our first enquiry, the quality must be up to the sample we sent you, and the weight and colour of the cotton insulation identical to that of the sample. Our order is placed on these conditions.

Yours faithfully

## [2] *Exporter's order for cloth, subject to price reduction*

Dear Sirs

Thank you for your quotation of 75p per metre for cloth no. 110.

Before we place an order with you, we would like to know whether you can quote us a slightly better price for the material. We are thinking in terms of an order for some 2,000 metres, and as the cloth is for export to a highly competitive market, a keen price is essential.

A prompt reply would be greatly appreciated.

Yours faithfully

## [3] *Exporter's request for lower price*

Dear Sirs

We have received your quotation of 1 February and the samples of men's suitings we asked for, and thank you for these.

While we appreciate the good quality of your products, we find the prices of these materials rather high for the market we supply. We have to point out that very good materials of this type are being exported by European manufacturers at prices from 10% to 15% below yours, so the prices you quote would make it impossible for us to compete on the market in question.

We would like to place our order with you, but must ask you to consider making us a more favourable offer. As our order would be worth around £8,000, you may find a concession worthwhile.

Yours faithfully

[4] *Rejection of offer of coffee* *(Reply to letter no. 8, page 29)*

Dear Sirs

We thank you for your letter of 21 November, in which you offer us Brazilian coffee at 60p per kg.

We are sorry to tell you that we cannot take you up on this, as the price you are asking is above the market level here for the quality in question. The coffee we bought from the same source last year was not of the quality we had expected for the price quoted.

Yours faithfully

[5] *Dealer asks for guaranteed delivery date* *(Reply to letter no. 5, page 27)*

---

# L. THOMS & SON

*Hardware Merchants*

150 Beachview Avenue
Bournemouth H77 6DP

30 January 1978

Modern Plastics Ltd.
Melox House
Portsmouth P92 4CC

Dear Sirs

Thank you for your letter of 12 January and for the details of your plastic ware.

We have now seen samples of your products and are prepared to give them a trial, provided you can guarantee delivery on or before 1 March. The enclosed order is placed strictly on this condition, and we reserve the right to cancel and to refuse delivery after this date.

Yours faithfully
L. THOMS AND SON

J.B.K. Thoms
Managing Director

---

Now we will turn to the seller and pick up the transaction from his point of view. The order has been received, and the usual practice is to acknowledge it at once. With small routine orders from regular customers this may be done by means of a ready-printed postcard. This tells the buyer that his order has been received and is receiving attention; in addition, it saves time and unnecessary correspondence.

More satisfactory is a letter in which the acknowledgement takes the form of a repetition of the order. This serves as a check on the accuracy of the description of the goods ordered and turns the order into a firm contract.

In all other cases, a polite letter of acknowledgement is obviously good policy. The seller started by expressing his intention of serving his customer when he made his first offer; it is only common sense to show that he appreciates being given the business. This need not take long, but the letter should refer to the actual goods ordered and the terms agreed; it should close with an assurance that the order will be carefully attended to and promptly delivered. Of course, the seller will only do this if he is as good as his word. A promise made must be kept, if he wants to keep his customer. There would be no point in sending out letters of this kind if he proceeded to treat the matter in a casual way: it would become known in time that his letters were a mere formality.

## [6] *Manufacturer acknowledges order and guarantees delivery*

Dear Sirs

Thank you very much for your order of 2 March for:

5 doz. tea services no. 53.
3 ,,   dinner services no. 65.
4 gross cups and saucers, export seconds, white.

All these items are in stock, and we can guarantee delivery to your Liverpool warehouse well before 15 March. As requested, we will advise you of date of despatch.

We are at your service at all times.

Yours faithfully

## [7] *Manufacturer acknowledges order and confirms priority*

Dear Sir

We were very glad to receive your order for:

2 horizontal drilling machines,

to be supplied to your own specification.

As we mentioned in our previous letter, delivery for machines made to supplied specifications is not normally possible in less than 3 months, but we should like to help you and are giving your order priority. You may be sure that your machines will be ready for shipment by 1 April.

We will advise you when your order is ready for collection and shall be pleased to assist you to the best of our ability at all times.

Yours faithfully

44

r Sirs

nk you for your interest in our special offer of tinned beef, and are pleased to
ou that your order has been despatched today by Road Transport Services, Ltd.

fully

ry much for your order for:

chines—catalogue no. 79/B.

despatched immediately upon receipt of your remittance for £375, as per
forma invoice.

y

## [10] *The sellers promise punctual despatch*

Dear Sirs

Many thanks for your order of 3 March for:

2,000 litres assorted distempers.

It is already being attended to and there will be no difficulty in getting the goods to you by your stipulated date.

Yours faithfully

### *Assuring the customer of your attention*

62. You may rely on us to carry out your instructions in every detail.
63. Your order is receiving immediate attention and you can depend on us to effect delivery at Southampton well within your time limit.
64. We have taken special note of your packing instructions and these will be strictly observed.
65. Special instructions have been given to our despatch department to send your orders on 1 May, 1 June and 1 July respectively. You may be sure that your wishes will be carried out.
66. We note that the goods are to be collected at our works by your forwarding agent, and we shall accordingly notify Carter & Sons when the order is ready to be called for.
67. We cannot guarantee delivery by next Friday as your order was received too late for this week's despatch, but we are sending your goods by rail, and they will reach you more quickly than if we waited for the next van delivery.

### *Execution of orders*

68. The goods are nearly ready for despatch and we should be glad to have your instructions.
69. We have not yet had precise shipping instructions and are holding your order until these arrive.
70. As you do not give any special instructions for forwarding, we are passing your order to our forwarding agents in the usual way.
71. As you need the goods so urgently we have arranged transport by road to the port. This will make shipment by *S.S. Dinard* possible.
72. To avoid storage charges at the port, we are holding your goods here pending arrival of your forwarding instructions.

See also *Shipping and Forwarding*, Chapter 8

## *Mentioning method of payment*

73. Please inform us what arrangements you have made for payment. Shipment will be effected immediately we have your reply.
74. As we have not had the pleasure of doing business with you before, we enclose a copy of our invoice, and will be glad if you will arrange payment either by banker's draft or by opening an irrevocable letter of credit in our favour. Please also state what documents you require.
75. In view of the urgent nature of your order we suggest that you arrange payment by banker's transfer, confirmed to us by telegraph.
76. As requested, we shall draw on you at 60 days for the amount of our invoice, one copy of which is enclosed, the draft to be accepted by your bankers as arranged.

See also *Payments*, Chapter 7

## *Prices and payment queries—replies*

77. Our terms are net. You will appreciate that our low prices make it impossible for us to grant any discount.
78. We are grateful to you for the order, but regret we cannot allow a further discount of 5% as requested.
.79. Our prices are ex-works; should you wish us to undertake shipping arrangements we will gladly do so, adding the costs involved to our draft on you.
80. We are accepting your order at the prices quoted in our letter, but cannot guarantee that they will hold good for further orders.
81. Prices of raw materials have risen steeply since our quotation of 1 May, and we could now accept your order only at the rates quoted on the attached list. We await your confirmation before executing your order, but shall be pleased to give you priority if your reply reaches us within 3 days.

See also *Banking and Payments*, Chapter 9

## [11] *Price concession agreed* (Reply to letter no. 2, page 42)

Dear Sirs

Many thanks for your letter of 18 May, in which you ask us for a keener price for our pattern 110.

Much as we would like to help you in the market you mention in your letter, we do not think there is room for a reduction in our quotation as we have already cut our price in anticipation of a substantial order. At 75p per metre this cloth competes well with any other product of its quality on the home or foreign markets.

We are willing, however, to offer you a discount of 5% on future orders of value £5,000 or over, and this may help you to develop your market. Meanwhile we will execute your present order with this concession, and we await your acceptance of this offer.

Yours faithfully

## [12] *Price reduction refused* (Reply to letter no. 3, page 42)

Dear Sirs

Many thanks for your letter of 5 February. We have now given careful consideration to your comments on our offer of men's suitings.

We are keen, of course, to meet your wishes and to supply you with material which will enable you to compete in Eastern markets, but regret that any reduction in the prices quoted is not possible at present. The qualities offered are the finest available at these prices, and considerably better than those of foreign makers who supply the markets you mention.

We think you would do better to order wool mixtures nos. 31–50 in our pattern-book, and we are arranging for our representative to call to discuss these with you, as they are ideal for your market and the prices are right.

We will do our very best for you.

Yours faithfully

## [13] *Manufacturer informs customer that goods are ready for despatch*

Dear Sirs

We have pleasure in informing you that your order no. 844772 has been completed and is awaiting collection. The consignment consists of 5 crates, each weighing 255 kg.

Transport, insurance and freight are being arranged by our forwarding agents, Heinz Lederer AG of Hamburg. We can vouch for their expertise and efficiency.

As soon as we receive details of forwarding charges from our agents, we will send you our invoice and the shipping documents. The amount of the invoice will be charged to your account, and in future we will draw on you quarterly, as previously agreed.

We assure you that your orders will be given prompt attention, and look forward to hearing from you again.

Yours faithfully

## *Delays in execution of orders*

You will not find the acknowledging of orders and the advising of despatch very difficult when you have studied the specimen letters and phrases given in this and other chapters. But explaining matters such as delays in despatch, inability to supply the goods ordered, or possibly even accepting an order, calls for a little more care in phrasing:

82. Much to our regret, your order has been held up at the docks by a strike of stevedores. You will appreciate that these circumstances are beyond our control.
83. Owing to delays in the delivery of raw materials, we fear we may be unable to execute your order before 23 January. Please accept our apologies for the inconvenience caused—we are working to capacity to catch up with schedule.
84. A slight delay in the execution of your order will now be unavoidable, but we are giving it priority and you will not have to wait more than 3 days longer than the original delivery date. We regret this and can only hope that it will not seriously inconvenience you.
85. The recent exceptional demand for this line makes it impossible to promise delivery of any further orders before 15 June.
86. We very much regret that our earliest delivery date is now 1 January, as we find it impossible to keep pace with the rush of orders this season. Will you kindly confirm your order for this date.
87. We think it fair to point out that recent changes in import quotas may cause us difficulty in executing contract orders and that some delay is inevitable.

## [14] *Apology for delay by strike*

Dear Sirs

The recent strike of transport workers here has caused delays in the despatch of a number of our export orders, and we regret that yours, too, is temporarily held up.

Your order was despatched from here 2 days ahead of the guaranteed time, and we are told that the goods are now in London awaiting shipment. We are making private arrangements for their transport to the docks and should be able to get them on the next ship, which sails on 3 March.

We apologise for this unfortunate delay and are doing our utmost to get your order away.

Yours faithfully

## [15] *Delay caused by Government regulations*

Dear Sirs

We are very sorry indeed to have to advise you of a delay in executing your order no. . . . of . . .

As you may know, the Government has recently put an embargo on the free export of certain metals to the Far East and we have to obtain a special licence to proceed with your order. We think the delay will not be more than 2–3 weeks, and we shall give your order priority as soon as we receive authority to go ahead. Meanwhile, please accept our apologies for the inconvenience caused.

Yours faithfully

## *Refusing an order*

88. We will be unable to accept any more orders for this item until further notice.
89. Regarding item no. 6 of your order, we regret that we do not manufacture this in stainless steel.
90. In this instance we are unable to accept your order, as we cannot match your pattern.
91. Much as we should like to do business with you, we fear we cannot turn out brushes of reasonable quality at the price you ask.
92. Supplies of raw materials are becoming difficult to obtain and we have no alternative but to decline your order.
93. As our factory is at present fully occupied with contract orders, we regret having to decline your order.
94. As we would not be able to promise delivery before next spring, we feel we must return your order, with our apologies and thanks.
95. We have a waiting list of several hundred for these machines and can give no guarantee of delivery this year.
96. Production difficulties force us to decline further orders for this model for the time being.
97. The political situation has caused supplies of bristle to 'dry up' entirely, and we are forced to discontinue the manufacture of these pure bristle goods.
98. There is no demand for material of the type you submit as a sample, and we shall not manufacture further supplies.
99. Any alteration in design would mean re-setting our machines, and the cost of this would be prohibitive unless you could place an order for some 5,000.
100. It would be impossible for us to supply this small quantity in wrappers of varying design and colour, without considerably raising the prices.
101. It would not be possible to produce economically the small quantity you require.

102. While thanking you for your order, we have to explain that we supply only to authorised dealers in each town, and at present we are not considering increasing the number of dealers in your area.
103. We are at present supplying only to wholesalers, and therefore refer you to Messrs. . . ., who would be pleased to supply your needs.
104. We are obliged to you for your order, which we have passed to our agents, Messrs. Smith & Co., Cape Town, for attention.

## [16] *Manufacturer is forced to refuse an order for technical reasons*

Dear Sirs

We thank you very much for the order contained in your letter of 20 December.

After carefully considering it, however, we have come to the conclusion that it would be better for you to approach another manufacturer in this instance. To machine to the limits required in your specification would require the setting up of special equipment at our works, and this would not only be impossible before September, but would seriously interrupt our normal production.

We are really sorry not to be more helpful, but hope that you will understand our position. Do let us have other enquiries at any time, as we shall be only too pleased to meet you if it is within our power.

Yours faithfully

## [17] *Seller refuses to supply on buyer's terms*

Dear Sirs

We are very grateful to you for your indent no. 32 for 10,000 boxes of paper fasteners.

To our regret, we are unable to accept your order at the price requested: £25 per 1,000. You will find on referring to our previous correspondence (21 June last) that we gave you our lowest price for this quantity as £27 per 1,000. Since then, prices have tended to rise rather than fall, and our profit margin does not warrant any concession by way of quantity reduction or discount.

We should, of course, be glad to fulfil your order if you will confirm at £27 per 1,000, settlement at 30 days.

Yours faithfully

## *Refusals—closing sentences*

105. As soon as we are in a position to supply this line we will get in touch with you again.
106. Our difficulties are only temporary, and we will welcome your orders in the future.
107. We hope you will understand the circumstances which compel us to decline your order this time, and that you will contact us again in the near future.
108. We are extending our works and installing new plant, so that we will not again have to refuse orders such as yours.
109. You may rely on us to inform you as soon as we are able to supply these goods again.
110. We are confident that supplies of raw materials will be readily available within the next few weeks, and this will enable us to resume production. We will be getting in touch with you as soon as the situation is back to normal.
111. We think that the current industrial dispute will be brought to a speedy end, and will contact you as soon as a solution has been reached.

## SUBSTITUTES AND COUNTER OFFERS

Of course, it is not always necessary to refuse an order. A sensible firm will only do so in cases where either they simply cannot supply anything like the required goods or, for their own good reasons, they do not want the business.

If they receive an order for something they cannot supply, there are two courses open to them:

(*a*) Send a substitute.

(*b*) Make a counter-offer.

Sending a substitute carries the risk that the buyer may be annoyed or even refuse it (in international trade it is also a violation of commercial practice). The whole thing is a matter of judgement. With a regular customer one may be reasonably safe in sending the nearest one has to what he wants (i.e. a substitute).

In other cases the question of the urgency of the customer's need may help the seller to decide whether to send a substitute, make a counter-offer or regretfully decline the order. A counter-offer is an offer of other goods or services which are not precisely what the customer asks for. The seller may make a counter-offer rather than risk sending a substitute.

Of course, there are limits to how far one can go in making counter-offers, and the desire to satisfy a customer must be as much in the seller's mind as the desire to get the sale. If the customer shows clearly that he knows what he wants, it may not be so easy to convince him.

Here, however, is how one exporter puts his counter-offer:

[18] *An exporter offers a new model instead of an earlier one he is unable to supply*

Dear Sirs

It was a pleasure to receive your order for 300 Model C 'Reflex' cameras and to hear of your success in disposing of the last consignment. As we advised you at the time of your last purchase, this type of camera, with its large viewfinder, has become a best-selling model, and you cannot go wrong in stocking it.

While sales throughout the world have been good, there has been a persistent demand for a lens of larger aperture than the f6.3, which was fitted as standard on the Model C last year. On careful examination of this demand we came to the conclusion that the average camera-user of today wants an instrument with which he can do serious picture-making. We have therefore produced a new version of our famous camera—the Model D, which is fitted with an f4.5 lens.

Model 'D' has replaced 'C', and at a price of DM 80 net to the trade, represents the finest value on the market for cameras of this type. We think you will agree that the difference in price, DM 10, between this and the old model is very small for the amazing difference in performance which is now possible. It has received an enthusiastic welcome here already.

Our new publicity campaign is due to begin in a few weeks and the 'D' Reflex will be advertised extensively in national newspapers in your country as well as in technical magazines. Your stock will reach you in good time for the commencement of our campaign, so we should be glad if you would confirm the order for 300 of Model 'D' in place of the discontinued Model 'C'.

We shall be happy to grant you an extra 5% discount for 300, and can promise you immediate despatch. Once again we say you cannot go wrong with a Reflex.

We are always at your service.

Yours faithfully

## [19] *Counter-offer of silk at a higher price*

Dear Sirs

Very many thanks for your letter of yesterday, enclosing your order for 1,000 metres of 'Willow' pattern silk cloth.

In turning to us for a supply of this famous line, you evidently realise that if such an article is to be had at all, we are the people to supply it. We appreciate your interest, and would have liked to be able to supply your order from stock as we did years ago.

However, times and tastes change. The 'Willow' pattern is now out of fashion, and in common with other manufacturers we have so little demand for it that we have ceased to produce it.

We think, however, that your customers would like our new material 'Rayon Porcellan', a sample of which we have pleasure in sending you with this letter. This material has all the good qualities of the old 'Willow' pattern and is very much smarter in appearance, without being as vivid in colour as many modern silks and rayons.

The price is 83p per metre or £41 per 50-metre piece, f.o.b. Liverpool. Prices for all silk fabrics have increased considerably in the past year and it is no longer possible to supply a really good material at the figure you name. As you know, we supply only first-class and guaranteed fabrics.

A full selection of our silk patterns is also being sent you by parcel post. All of these are selling well in your country and we can safely recommend them to you.

We can ship your order within a week of hearing from you.

Yours faithfully

*To end this chapter here is a further selection of sentences to use in making counter-offers or sending substitutes:*

112. We cannot supply exactly to your order as . . .
113. . . . our stock is completely exhausted.
114. . . . these designs are out of fashion.
115. . . . we do not stock the sizes required.
116. . . . these colours are no longer available.
117. We can offer you instead . . .
118. We recommend you to buy a synthetic material such as . . .
119. Quality 15X is equally (hard wearing) (waterproof) (damp-resisting) (acid-proof) (attractive) (serviceable).
120. It is no longer possible to obtain supplies of this material, but the very similar article X is in good supply.
121. We strongly advise you to accept catalogue no. 32, as the model you selected is no longer obtainable.
122. We could not guarantee to keep within the price-limit set by you and must ask you for a little latitude in this respect.

123. Our price was quoted for orders of £1,000 and over, and we must ask you to increase your order to this figure if you wish to profit by the lower price.
124. As our prices apply only for quantities of 1 dozen, we have sent you 12 of each, and trust that this will meet with your approval.
125. We have had to increase our prices since you last ordered.
126. We have been compelled to raise our prices by 10% owing to . . .
127. . . . increased labour costs.
128. . . . the rise in raw material prices.
129. . . . heavier import duties on raw materials.
130. . . . rising freight and transport costs.
131. If your market will stand an extra 10p per bottle we can offer you . . .
132. If you can raise your order to 1,000 we can offer you a price of Fr. 2.30 each.

## Substitutes

133. We have substituted surface no. 5 (Smooth Lustre) for no. 4 (Half Lustre), as the latter is no longer available in cream.
134. As your order is marked URGENT, we have sent you type XX, which is the nearest we can supply at present. We hope you will approve.
135. Following several complaints, we have withdrawn these chemicals from stock and are substituting with 'AL' brand in your consignment.
136. As prices are low in the London market, we sent your fruit to Bristol, where a price nearer that which you hoped for was obtained.
137. We can obtain the knives at the price you want only with celluloid handles. Please telex us immediately if you wish to purchase these.
138. We would like your confirmation before supplying so large a quantity in the alternative designs now proposed.
139. As size 5 cm. × 8 cm. is no longer manufactured, we are sending 6 cm. × 9 cm. as a substitute.
140. We cannot quite match the finish of your sample, but are sending you our nearest.

## Some vocabulary of Chapter 5

*alternative*: Another possibility.
*bear in mind*: Remember, consider.
*content*: Proportion, percentage.
*contents*: What is contained in something.
*discretion*: Judgement.
*extend* (*v.*): To make longer or larger. (*n.*) extension; (*adj.*) extensive.
*indent*: Order, one of a series of orders from a regular customer.
*in the right frame of mind*: Contented, in a good mood.
*keen competition*: Hard competition.
*keen price*: Competitive price.
*we are keen to help you*: We are eager to help you.
*keep it for further reference*: Keep it so that we can consult it later.
*match*: Be similar to, harmonise with.
*much as we would like*: Although we would like.
*observance of*: Paying attention to; acting in accordance with.
*pending*: Awaiting.
*reject* (*v.*): To refuse to accept.
52

*seconds*: Goods which cannot be sold as perfect.
*slump*: Rapid fall.
*substitute*: Alternative offered if the article ordered is not available.
*vouch for*: To express confidence in.


EXERCISES

1. Fill in the missing words:

   Our order _____ 50 'Marie' dresses _____ various colours and sizes is _____ with this letter. You will see _____ the order that _____ is required _____ 1 May _____ the latest.

   Will you please quote us _____ 100 'Audrey' dressing gowns, and _____ us know whether you have these models _____ stock.

2. Write a letter based on these notes:

   thanks for order (no., date)—goods despatched (ship, date due)—invoice enclosed—goods carefully selected—packed crates—safe arrival—excellent value—hope good sales—rely on us—at your service.

3. Write a letter to a foreign manufacturer of some article you are familiar with. Enclose an order and state your requirements regarding quantity, quality, appearance and delivery.

4. The Government of your country has now removed an embargo on the import of certain luxury goods. Write a letter to an exporter in a foreign country and order a selection of his goods. Mention alternative goods, terms and delivery dates.

5. Write an answer to letter no. 1 of this chapter.

6. Send a reply to letter no. 2 of this chapter.

7. Send a reply to letter no. 5 of this chapter.

8. Your firm has received an order for machine tools from an overseas buyer. Write a letter of acknowledgement and promise delivery by a certain date.

9. You have received an order for a brand which you no longer export. Write an answer, explaining why you are unable to supply the article in question, and offering a substitute.

10. Your company has received an order based on an out-of-date price list. Prices have since been increased by 10%–15%. Write a reply.

11. Acknowledge an order for cotton textiles and explain why a slight delay in execution is unavoidable.

12. Write a letter to a firm which has often supplied your company with tinned food products. Say why you have to refuse their latest offer.

13. Your firm has despatched goods ordered by a buying agent and has sent substitutes for several items. Write a letter of explanation to the agent.

14. You have received an order for a piece of machinery, but your firm has recently sold the last one in stock. You will not be able to supply for about three months, but you have another machine at a higher price in stock.

    (a) Write a suitable letter to your customer.

    (b) Write the customer's answer, refusing your offer.

15. Reply to letter no. 19 of this chapter, placing a trial order and insisting on early delivery.

# 6 | Packing and despatch

Anyone who has ever tried to pack a Christmas parcel and who has known the frustration that this seemingly simple operation can entail will agree that packing is an art. So badly is it often done that by the time the parcel reaches its destination it may be reduced to a shapeless mass by the not very gentle handling it has received on its journey. Only really 'healthy' parcels come through the ordeal of transport unscathed.

The real art of packing is to get the contents into a nice, compact shape that will stay that way during the roughest journey, and wrap the lot with a good strong cover of some kind. Somewhere between the thin brown paper parcel that tears open at the first touch and the heavy box that gets there all right but costs more in postage than the contents are worth, lies the happy medium that makes the whole thing practical.

This, on a large scale, is the problem that faces the despatch department of every firm, especially the export firm. The buyer has a right to expect that his goods will reach him in perfect condition, and the seller has to pack them in such a way that they will do so. Nothing is more infuriating to a buyer than to find his goods damaged, or part missing on arrival: and nothing is more likely to lose a customer. In the export trade serious delays may result, causing the customer great loss. It is because of these dangers that large export firms have established a special department for export packing, and the whole question is under regular review. New packing materials are being developed which are light and strong, and new methods being found to ensure the safe transport of heavier goods. Many export firms employ a specialist export packer or forwarding agent to do their packing for them.

The general plan in all packing is to make the goods secure for the kind of journey they have to make, but to keep the package as small and light as possible. Transport costs on land usually depend on the weight, but on the sea the size of the package is also important.

For correspondence, you will find the following list of specialised terms useful:

## Ⓐ PACKING CONTAINERS

*Bag* Generally made of paper, linen, canvas, rubber, or plastic.
*Sack* A larger, stronger version of a bag, usually made of jute.

**Carton**  
Made of light but strong cardboard, or fibreboard, it has double lids and bottoms which are fixed together. Sometimes several cartons are made up into a single package, held by metal bands.

**Box**  
Stronger than a carton, made of wood, cardboard or metal, sometimes with a folding (hinged) lid.

**Case**  
A strong container made of wood. For extra strength, cases may have *battens* fixed to their tops, bottoms and sides. When thin wood is used, metal bands or wires will be passed around the case. Cases are often *lined* with various materials to prevent damage by water, air, insects, etc.

**Crate**  
This is like a case, but is not fully enclosed. It has a bottom and a frame, and is sometimes open at the top. Crates are often built for the particular thing they have to carry. Machinery packed in crates needs a special bottom, called a *skid*, to facilitate handling.

**Container**  
A very large, robust, metal construction, varying in length from about ten to about forty feet. It is normally sealed at the consignor's factory and transported unopened until it reaches its destination. Containers are carried by rail, road and by ship. They may be watertight and airtight, and goods sent in them cannot be lost or stolen. Containers are a recent development, and they can make transportation very economical.

**Drum**  
A cylindrical container for liquids and powders, usually made of metal or plastic, but sometimes wood or strong cardboard.

56

| Barrel | A wooden drum. Hoops are used to strengthen barrels. There are various sizes of barrels, and some are known as *casks*, *hogsheads* and *kegs.* |  |
|---|---|---|
| Bale | A package of soft goods (usually textiles) wrapped in protective material. | |
| Tin (U.S.A. *can*) | A small metal container which paint, oil and a variety of foodstuffs are packed in. | |
| Carboy | A glass container, used for chemicals, protected in a padded metal or wicker cage. |  |
| Bundle | Miscellaneous goods packed without a container. | |

## B TERMS USED IN CONNECTION WITH DESPATCH AND TRANSPORT OF GOODS

See also *Shipping and Forwarding*, Chapter 8

**Packaging**
to pack; airtight; battened; bolted; braced; cleated; covering material; filling material; insulated; lining; locked; nailed; padding; screwed; sealed; waterproof; wrapping

**Despatch**
to consign; to despatch; to send; bulk; capacity; dimensions; gross weight; mass; net weight; space; volume; weight

**Transport**
carriage; cartage; carter; charges; dues; freight; load; lorry; lorry-load; overland; rail; railway; road; transport; to transport; truck; van; barge; canal; lighter; to tow; in tow; on tow; towage; tug; waterway

**At the docks**
chain; crane; derrick; hook; lifting gear; porter; ship-load; sling; stevedore; tackle; to discharge; to load; to unload; to stack; to stow

57

# C. SPECIMEN SENTENCES: INSTRUCTION AND INFORMATION ON PACKING, ETC.

## [1] *Supplier's information to customer*

1. The 0·5 litre size tins of paint will be supplied in strong cardboard cartons, each containing 48 tins. Gross weight 50 kg. The 1 litre size will be packed in cartons of 24, also of gross weight 50 kg.
2. All powders are wrapped in polythene bags and packed in tins, the lids of which are sealed with adhesive tape.
3. Fibreboard boxes are used to reduce freight. These boxes are not returnable.
4. We supply sulphate crystals in 50 kg. and 100 kg. sacks of impregnated jute, so that contamination during transport is unlikely.
5. All bags have an inner waterproof lining.
6. We supply these machines in specially designed crates. If not returned to us within 3 weeks, the crates are charged to you at £5 each.
7. All export bicycles are wrapped in strong waterproof material at the port and packed in pairs in lightweight crates.
8. A special crate with reinforced bottom will be needed for the transport of such a large machine, and both padding and bolting down will be essential. The cost would be in the region of £20 plus total freight charges of £25.
9. To save freight we suggest packing in a crate with reinforced base, and overall waterproof wrapping. A solid case as proposed by you would be uneconomical.
10. Export crates for goods of the type you name are completely enclosed by plywood, and firmly battened.
11. Partial boarding of the crate will save freight and give ample protection to the contents.
12. Export orders are put up in strong cases, cleated and wire-strapped. Solid packing and stuffing inside the cases gives protection from vibration and jarring.
13. A light case reinforced by battens would meet your requirements and be much cheaper than a solid wooden case, as the former would be non-returnable.
14. Carbon tetrachloride is supplied in 500 kg. drums. The drums are of steel, with double hooping as reinforcement.
15. These products are available in strong metal drums of 1, 2, 5, 10 and 20 litres.
16. The most economical size for you would be our 50 litre carboy. Carboys may be retained by you without charge for 2 months.
17. All preparations, chemicals, etc., are supplied in stout fibre drums of 50 kg. capacity, and wrapped in sealed polythene bags.
18. Pitch and tar are delivered in wooden barrels of capacity 200 litres.
19. We will pack the material in bales of size approx. 2 metres length and 3 metres girth. The protective canvas will be provided with ears to facilitate lifting.
20. When the various items of your order are complete in our warehouse we will pack them into bundles of suitable size for shipment.
21. Your poles will leave here in bundles of 61, wrapped in sacking and firmly clamped by wire bands.

## [2] *Customer's instructions to supplier*

22. We do not object to packing in cartons, provided the flaps are glued down and the cartons secured by metal bands.
23. Please limit the weight of any one carton to 15 kg. and metal-strap all cartons in stacks of 4.
24. If cartons are used, please supply each chemical in strong polythene bags to ensure protection from damp.

25. Please sort the smaller metal parts in canvas bags before packing in the crate.
26. Please wrap each item separately in grease-paper.
27. Crates must not exceed an overall length of 3 metres.
28. The bottom and back of the crate must be strongly boarded.
29. Packing in sturdy wooden cases is essential. Cases must be nailed, battened and secured by overall metal strapping.
30. Valves and all delicate parts are to be wrapped in soft material and firmly packed in cardboard boxes. These in turn are to be packed in cases in such a manner that movement inside the cases is impossible.
31. Cases must have an inner lining of stout, damp-resisting paper.
32. The packets must be made up in piles of suitable size before being given their air-tight tinfoil cover, and then packed in cases. The cases must be cleated and battened so as to eliminate the risk of damage by pressure.
33. Please cut vent-holes in the cases to minimise condensation.
34. Overall measurements of each case must not exceed 1·5m. × 1m. × 1m.
35. Please supply 4 carboys, heavily padded and packed in a single crate.
36. Please make our order up into bales of about 200 kg., covered with waterproof fabric and strapped vertically and horizontally with metal bands.

## [3] *General instructions from customer to supplier*

37. When packing, please take into account that the boxes are likely to receive rough handling at this end and must be able to withstand transport over very bad roads.
38. We give you on the attached sheet full details regarding packing and marking. These must be strictly observed.
39. The greatest care must be given to packing and crating, as any damage in transit would cause us heavy loss.
40. Please convey the finished goods by your own transport to our forwarding agent's warehouse, where they will be repacked for shipment.
41. When packing is complete, please notify our agents, Messrs. . . .
42. Please use normal export containers unless you receive special instructions from our agents.
43. As the goods will probably be subjected to a thorough customs examination, the cases should be of a type which can easily be made fast again after opening.
44. Tanks must be completely drained of fuel before the vehicles are crated, and all oil removed from sumps.
45. All polished parts of the machine are to be wrapped and generously padded to avoid scratching and knocking against the container.
46. Rope or metal handles should be fixed to the boxes to facilitate carrying. No grip-holes must be left in the boxes.

## [4] *Despatch*

See also *Shipping and Forwarding*, Chapter 8

47. We are pleased to advise you that your order no. 32 has been despatched, packed in 12 100 kg. cases, in accordance with your instructions.
48. As requested, we have included a packing note with your goods, and have pleasure in enclosing a further copy of the note.
49. Your order for shipment per *S.S. Dover Castle* on 3 March was collected yesterday by your forwarding agent.
50. We have pleasure in informing you that your order is now ready for despatch, and we await your instructions.
51. Your goods were despatched this morning, carriage forward as requested.

52. In view of the urgency of the order, we have despatched it today by train, so that the goods should reach you tomorrow.
53. We enclose our pro-forma invoice, on settlement of which your order will be despatched without delay.
54. We have today executed that part of your order which we could supply from stock. The remainder may be subject to a delay of three to six weeks. Our invoice for the goods despatched is enclosed.
55. Your order has been despatched by road transport to avoid risks of frequent handling.
56. The enclosed invoice shows a charge of £3 each for carboys. The amount involved will be credited to you on receipt of the returned empties.
57. Our packing charge includes £1 for the drum, which sum will be credited on return.
58. Please return empties, carriage forward, to our depot.
59. Cartons are not charged and are not returnable.

## MARKING

There are 3 principal types of marking which may have to be done on export packages:
1. The consignees' own distinctive marks.
2. Any official mark required by authorities.
3. Special directions or warnings.

In addition, weights and dimensions may be required.

Good clear marking is essential if the goods are not to go astray, and for this reason marks are usually made by paint, inks or dyes through a metal stencil. Wooden cases are sometimes marked by burned impressions in the wood itself.

Under 1 we have the shippers' or importers' own marks, which are registered and so serve as identification. These marks are as important to the many people engaged in shipping as the address on an envelope is to the postman. They include the name of the port of destination.

Under 2 we have special marks demanded by the country of export or import. Some countries require the name of the country of origin of the goods to be marked on every package, and weights and dimensions may also be required.

Under 3 we have some special instructions regarding manner of handling, loading, lifing, etc., and various warnings both for the owner's and the carrier's benefit.

*Specimens of marks*

**1**

| K  R    |          | X    X    |
|---------|----------|-----------|
| Durban  | LTV      |           |
|         | X        | 3         |
|         | Brisbane | Singapore |

**2**

| FOREIGN      |          | PRODUCE OF SOUTH AFRICA       |
|--------------|----------|-------------------------------|
| Net weight   | 100 kg.  | Dimensions                    |
| Gross weight | 125 kg.  | 1m. × 1.5m. × 2.25m.          |
| Tare         | 25 kg.   |                               |

60

## 3

THIS SIDE UP *deze kant boven*

FRAGILE *breekbaar*

STOW AWAY FROM HEAT

USE NO HOOKS

TO BE KEPT COOL

DO NOT DROP

GLASS WITH CARE

PERISHABLE *bederf houdbaar*

TOP *bovenkant*

KEEP DRY *droog bewaren*

ACID—WITH CARE *zuur - met zorg behandelen*

OPEN THIS END *a deze kant openen*

DO NOT STOW ON DECK *niet op het dek plaatsen*

INFLAMMABLE *ontvlambaar*

LIFT HERE *hier optichten*

HANDLE WITH CARE *met zorg behandelen*

In the past it very often happened that even clearly marked containers were roughly handled or wrongly stored—simply because the stevedores loading or unloading them could not understand the directions and warnings! For this reason the practice has developed of stencilling symbols representing warnings and directions: these can be understood by speakers of any language. Here are some examples:

(FRAGILE)          (USE NO HOOKS)          (RADIOACTIVE)

## Marking instructions

60. Please mark all cases XL Cape Town and send to our agents' warehouse at Funchal.
61. All boxes are to be marked as usual, but please number them consecutively from 1 to 11.
62. All marks other than our own and the name of country of origin are to be removed from the crates before shipment.
63. Kindly stencil our shipping marks in letters 10 cm. high, and give gross and net weight on each box.
64. We attach a list of marks and numbers for the various packages. Please give great care to clear and correct marking.

## Supplier's confirmation of execution

65. Your instructions as to marking have been accurately carried out and the goods packed with all the care of our experienced despatch staff.
66. We are pleased to confirm that your instructions regarding packing and marking have been accurately executed by our forwarding agents in London.

To conclude this chapter, here is a letter which incorporates some of the vocabulary already explained and illustrated in the phrases and sentences:

*Exporter informs prospective customer of packing and marking procedures*

# KAVEXPORT LENINGRAD

6 June 1977

Ascheim y Negrín SA
Diputación 235
Asunción
Paraguay

Dear Sirs

We thank you for your letter of 20 May, and can confirm that we are still offering our range of luxury foods at the prices quoted in our initial offer to you.

We understand your concern with packing, and can assure you that we take every possible precaution to ensure that our products reach our customers all over the world in prime condition.

For your information, "Ariel" caviar is packed as follows:

Each jar is wrapped in tissue paper before being placed in its individual decorative cardboard box. The boxes are then packed in strong cardboard cartons, twelve to a carton, separated from each other by corrugated paper dividers.

The cartons are then packed in strong wooden crates. Since the crates are specially made to hold twenty-four cartons, there is no danger of movement inside them. In addition, the crates are lined with waterproof, airtight material. The lids are secured by nailing, and the crates are strapped with metal bands.

In the case of consignments being sent to you, transhipment at Buenos Aires will be necessary, so each case will be marked with details required by the Argentinian authorities, as well as with your own mark, details of weights, etc., and symbols representing the following warnings and directions:

USE NO HOOKS, STOW AWAY FROM HEAT, and DO NOT DROP.

We hope this has answered your questions, and look forward to receiving orders from you.

Yours faithfully

*Some vocabulary of Chapter 6*

*facilitate* (*v.*): To make easier.

*medium* (*n.*): Half-way position, neutral between extremes ('happy medium').

*ordeal* (*n.*): Unpleasant or difficult experience. *beproeving*

*secure* (*adj.*): Safe, not in danger; (*v.*) secure. *veilig , beveiligen*

*unscathed* (*adj.*): Uninjured, undamaged, unmarked. *onbeschadigd*

## EXERCISES

1. You have seen samples of Finnish wine glasses at a trade fair, and would like to import a large quantity of them. However, you have heard that the manufacturer in question tends to pack his products rather carelessly, with the result that consignments often include large numbers of broken glasses. You have also heard that crates often arrive late because of insufficient marking.

   Discuss with your fellow-students how wine glasses should be packed, and then send an order to the Finnish manufacturer, giving detailed instructions as to how the goods are to be packed and the containers marked.

2. Write a letter for your firm to an English engineering firm, ordering a special machine. Give packing and marking instructions.

3. Send an order to a Swiss manufacturer of optical instruments, giving full packing instructions.

4. Describe how your firm wants its order for textiles packed. The goods are for export to a tropical country.

5. Answer an enquiry for industrial chemicals, quoting prices of various containers, sizes, and method of packing.

6. A cycle manufacturer has just despatched some bicycles and accessories to an overseas customer. Write the manufacturer's letter to the customer, telling the customer how the goods have been packed and marked, and how despatch has been effected.

# 7 | Invoicing, accounting and settlement of accounts

Accounting, banking and payments are subjects which have a vocabulary and phraseology of their own. When you have mastered these you will not have any great difficulty in writing the letters connected with them, for the principles of accounting and banking are almost universal. In this chapter we shall study only the correspondence connected with invoicing, accounting (i.e. book-keeping), terms of payment and simple payments.

When the customer's order is received by the manufacturer it is acknowledged by letter or postcard. (*See Chapter 5*) It is then passed for execution—by the Sales Manager or his department—and the work of packing the order can begin; or, in the case of goods not in stock, the order is sent to the factory for manufacture. In either case, there is paper-work to be done, as many of the manufacturer's departments (Sales, Accounts, Despatch, etc.) must have details of the order. A great deal of time and work is saved by the modern practice of using one kind of printed form for this purpose, copies in different colours being sent to the different departments. Details of the customer's name, goods ordered, order number, terms and any special instructions will be typed on this form, with space left for the price of the various items ordered. In this way, the accounts department can also use one of these copies as the *invoice*, or make out as many copies as are needed for a shipping order.

The invoice is an important document in the export trade, as copies may be required by banks, export/import agents, shipping companies, customs authorities, and consulates. It is therefore one of the shipping documents, and as there are other types of invoices, this one is called the commercial invoice.

Here are some of the terms and abbreviations connected with invoicing and accounting:

Dr. ( = Debit)                      Cr. ( = Credit)
a/c ( = account)                    c/f ( = carried forward)
b/f ( = brought forward)            Bal. ( = Balance)
c.w.o. ( = cash with order)         N/C ( = no charge)

The invoice will be sent to the customer by post, or through an agent or a bank. (*See Banking, Chapter 9*) In the case of single or isolated transactions, payment is then required, either before delivery or on delivery of the goods. This method of payment is called *payment on invoice*.

64

Here is a specimen British export invoice:

| Invoice To: | Invoice No: 3701 | Invoice Date 27 **January** 1979 | Country Code 10 |
|---|---|---|---|
| Bauer & Co. G.M.B.H. Kepplerstrasse 14, Frankfurt, Germany | Credit Note No | Credit Note Date | Our Bankers Lloyds Bank Ltd. Lombard Street, London EC3P 2BF |
| | Works No *fabrick* | Works Date | |
| Deliver To: | Customer Order No and Date | | Foreign Bank |
| Bauer & Co. Frankfurt via Hamburg | Delivery Date 20 **February** 1979 | Sight Draft Amount | |
| | Country of Origin G.B. | Credit Terms | |

| Quantity | Description | B.T.N. | Unit Price | TOTAL PRICE | |
|---|---|---|---|---|---|
| 12 dozen | Ash trays Model 294      per dozen | | £6 | 72 | 00 |
| 12 dozen | Cigarette lighters 'Flick Mk. 1'      per dozen | | £15 | 180 | 00 |
| | C.I.F. Hamburg | | | 252 | 00 |
| | *inhrous* (x3) | | | | |

| No and Kind of Packages | Gross Kg. | Nett Kg. | Size (Cms) | Cube |
|---|---|---|---|---|
| 1 case | 35 Kg | 15 Kg | 61 x 46 x 46 | *steam ship* |

| | | | Vessel/Flight SS **Brighton Belle** | Marks and Numbers |
|---|---|---|---|---|
| Forwarding Agent Biedermann Shipping Co. Ltd. | | A.W.B. | Date of Despatch 25 **January** 1979 | |
| | | Port of Loading London | Method of Despatch Road | |
| C.A.N. | Agents Ref/H.A.W.B. | Port of Discharge Hamburg | FREE CIRCULATION NON-FREE CIRCULATION | |

*you pay over a certain period*

But where the buyer has an open account with the seller, the latter will
not want payment on invoice. Instead he keeps a record of all invoices
sent out to his customer and then, once a month (or once a quarter) he will
send an account of all the goods despatched and payments received

during this period. This document is called the *statement* (i.e. statement of ~~rekening/~~
account—*see specimen on this page* and the customer knows that he now
has to pay. This is called *payment on statement*.

*Note:* A *pro-forma* invoice is a detailed statement of costs which is sent
to a buyer for information, and which must be paid before the goods are
delivered.

| | | |
|---|---|---|
| TELEPHONE<br>01·723·7720 | **STATEMENT** | TELEGRAMS:<br>"LEAPLAND" LONDON |

# Lea Price & Co. Ltd.

LONGLAND HOUSE, 20-25 HUNT STREET, LONDON EC 3P 2BE

Messrs. A J Smith Ltd.,
21/24, Stamford Street,
London, SE1 2BZ

DIRECTORS:
B. LEA
P. PRICE

-8 FEB 1979

| DATE | ITEM | FOLIO NO. | DEBIT | CREDIT | BALANCE |
|---|---|---|---|---|---|
| Jan. 1 | Account Rendered | | | | 20.67 |
| Jan. 3 | Invoice No. 27 | | 16.20 | | 36.87 |
| Jan. 7 | Invoice No. 42 | | 7.65 | | 44.52 |
| Jan. 10 | Invoice No. 61 | | 2.48 | | 47.00 |
| Jan. 13 | Credit No. 42A | | | 9.10 | 37.90 |
| Jan. 15 | Cash | | | 20.15 | |
| Jan. 15 | Discount | | | 0.51 | 17.24 |
| Jan. 29 | Invoice No. 103 | | 11.66 | | 28.90 |

PLEASE PAY THE LAST
AMOUNT SHOWN HERE

66

# METHODS OF PAYMENT IN FOREIGN TRADE

Accounts may be paid by means of:
(a) *International money order*: For small private transactions.
(b) *Banker's transfer*: Direct transfer from buyer's to seller's bank.
(c) *Bill of exchange:*
(d) *Letter of credit:* } *See Banking, Chapter 9.*

## Sending the invoice or statement

1. We enclose invoice amounting to £235.53, covering the first consignment per *S.S. Nova Scotia*.
2. The enclosed invoice in triplicate covers goods sent against your order no. . . .
3. We have pleasure in enclosing herewith our invoice to the amount of £57.09, on payment of which the order will be despatched.
4. On receipt of your remittance for DM 1150 we will release your order to the forwarders.
5. We enclose our pro-forma invoice as requested; all costs to Durban are included in it.
6. A copy of the invoice is enclosed. The shipping documents will be handed to you by the SAS Bank against settlement of the amount shown.
7. With this letter we are sending you a statement for January invoices totalling £235.
8. Our quarterly statement is enclosed, and the usual 2½% discount may be deducted if payment is effected by the last day of this month.
9. We have pleasure in enclosing our statement of account for all transactions up to 24 March. Please check the entries and if you find them correct, kindly carry forward the total of £ . . . to the April account.
10. Will you please let us have your cheque for the amount of the enclosed statement.
11. The balance of £100 left uncleared by your September payment has been brought forward to the enclosed statement for October and we would appreciate early settlement of the total amount now due.
12. Attached to this letter you will find our statement showing a balance of Fr. 2,523: we are drawing on you for this amount.

## Notifying payment of account

13. We enclose our (cheque) (money order) for £ . . . in settlement of your invoice no. 000 of 24 March.
14. We have pleasure in sending you enclosed our cheque for £ . . .
15. Thank you for prompt sending of the invoice. We have today transferred the amount of £123.38 to the XXZ Bank, London, for your credit.
16. Many thanks for your pro-forma invoice. We accept this price and are making immediate payment to our bank, . . ., who will notify you of the credit in due course.
17. Your statement of our account for the last quarter has been received and found correct. We have instructed our bank to remit the amount of £2,136.59 for the credit of your account at . . . Bank, London.
18. We are glad to advise you that your statement of our account as at June 30 corresponds with our books and we shall be pleased to accept your bill of exchange for this amount.
19. We have arranged payment through the PZX Bank in London of the sum of £1,000 . . .
20. . . . in settlement of your invoice no. 000.
21. . . . and ask you to credit our account accordingly.
22. . . . which clears our account, after allowing for discount at 2½%.
23. . . . which balances our account after taking into consideration credit note no. 000.

24. ... in part payment of your last statement.
25. ... in full settlement of your invoice.
26. ... as the first instalment under our agreement.
27. ... as a deposit against our order no. 000.
28. We have today instructed our bank, the YZY Corporation, to telegraph the amount due. Please acknowledge receipt.
29. The sum of £1,135 remitted yesterday through the XXX Bank clears our account up to 1 December. The balance will be sent on or before 31 December.

## ERRORS AND DISAGREEMENTS IN ACCOUNTS

### [1] *Error in totalling invoice*

Dear Sirs

With reference to your invoice no. 21026 of 3 July, we have to point out that you have made an error in your total. We calculate the correct figure at £237.73, not £247.73 as given by you.

Our cheque for the former amount is enclosed and we should be obliged if you would amend the invoice or pass the necessary credit.

Yours faithfully

### [2] *Error in extending item on invoice*

Dear Sirs

We thank you for prompt delivery of our order no. 212 of 3 May, and are pleased to report that the goods arrived in good condition.

Your invoice has now been received, and on checking this we find that you have made a mistake in the extension of item no. 3, 15 chairs at £3.35. You have extended this as £53.60, whereas the correct figure is £50.25. Please let us have your credit note for the difference.

Yours faithfully

### [3] *Disagreement on goods sent and charged*

Dear Sirs

Our indent no. 00265, your invoice no. 2345

The various items supplied against the above indent have now been checked and we regret to inform you that there is a discrepancy[i] between the goods sent and the amount invoiced.

Item no. 5 of our indent called for 10 × 6 men's poplin shirts, size L, and this quantity was in fact received. We noticed that your packing note showed 12 × 6 shirts against this item, and now we find that your invoice shows this quantity, too.

Will you kindly look into the matter and let us have your credit for the difference in due course.

Yours faithfully

### [4] *Incorrect discount in statement*

Dear Sirs

Your statement of account for the December quarter has been found in order but we think

68

you have made an error in the special discount shown. In your letter of 15 September last you agreed to allow us 5% extra on quarterly transactions exceeding £1,000 in value. The amount of the statement in question is £1,106, but you have shown discount at only 2½%.

Will you kindly adjust this, after which we shall be pleased to pass the account for payment.

Yours faithfully

## [5] Discrepancies in statement

We have received your statement for December 1978 and must point out certain discrepancies in your entries:

(1) 5 Dec. You debit us £55.38 against invoice no. 31752, but we have no record of such an invoice in our files, nor can we trace any packing note for goods that might explain this item.

(2) 19 Dec. Invoice no. 32101 for £31.50. This item is charged twice; as you will see, you have made a similar debit dated 29 December.

(3) Your final entry is 53p carriage² added to your entry for invoice no. 33711. We take it that this charge is made because the order in question is under £10 in value. While agreeing that you are entitled to make this charge, we think that the volume of business done with you in December should warrant³ a free delivery in this case.

Will you please let us have your comments.

## [6] Customer queries credits

Your quarterly statement arrived a few days ago and shows a balance in your favour of £527.40.

We have to draw your attention to two credit items which you do not show on this statement: firstly, an amount of £1.89 due to us in accordance with your credit note A124 of 17 May, and secondly, an amount of £5.83 due to us for empty crates and carboys returned to you on 30 April.

We have never had any credit note for the second of these two items, although we wrote to you on 5 June asking for credit.

Under these circumstances we are deducting a total of £7.72 from the amount of your statement and are instructing our bank to remit the sum of £519.64 in full settlement.

## [7] Seller's reply to letter no. 5

Dear Sirs,

Many thanks for your letter of . . . in which you query⁴ your current statement. We have examined our records carefully and have discovered that invoice no. 31752 of 5 December was charged to you in error and we enclose our credit note to the amount of £55.38 to adjust the matter.

We are very sorry indeed that you have been troubled.

Regarding your second query, we regret that the entry for 29 December was given against invoice no. 32101. This should read no. 32701, which invoice was also for the amount of £31.50. We think you will find that you did, in fact, receive these two lots of goods against your orders no. 37 and no. 55.

Finally, concerning the delivery charge of 53p for your order no. 60, this was quite properly made by our accounts department under standing instructions. However, we appreciate your business and are quite agreeable to waiving[5] the charge. Our further credit note to adjust the matter is enclosed.

We apologise for the inconvenience caused and look forward to doing further business with you.

Yours faithfully

## [8] *Seller complains of short payment*

We thank you for your remittance for £117.18 received today by our bank. Our official receipt is enclosed.

The amount of the statement in question is £157.18 and as you make no mention of this in your recent letters we are wondering if this is a clerical error[6] on your part.

Perhaps you would remit the balance of £40 in the course of the next few days.

## [9] *Seller rejects request for discount*

We thank you for your letter of . . . in which you draw our attention to an apparent error in the discount we have calculated on your quarterly statement dated 31 December.

Through an oversight, no accompanying letter went out with your statement. The position is that the discount of 5% agreed on orders over £1,000 was granted on condition that no balance was outstanding[7] from previous accounts. At the time of writing there is a balance of £300 due from our last account rendered, and under the circumstances we can only offer the normal 2½% discount.

You will appreciate that while we are anxious to give every assistance, we are only able to make discount concessions if accounts are cleared promptly.

# EXCHANGES, ADJUSTMENTS, ETC.

## [10] *Letter from an accounts department adjusting charges to a customer*

Dear Sirs

We apologise for the inconvenience caused by the delivery to you of two consignments of bromide developer which should have been shipped to another customer. Please accept our thanks for agreeing to keep the heavier of these two packages for your own account, to save freight; also for forwarding the smaller package to Messrs. J. H. B. To adjust your account we are debiting you with £11.13 for the bromide you have decided to keep, and crediting you with the sum of 75p, which we understand was the freight charge paid by you for the forwarding of the package to Messrs. J. H. B.

The matter has now been adjusted and we appreciate your co-operation.

Yours faithfully

## [11] *Adjustment of charges covering an exchange*

We attach our credit note for goods which you returned and which were supplied against your order no. 050. We understand that you wish to have pattern no. 000 in place of the returned items, and your instructions are receiving our attention.

The amount of £1.08 is being debited to your account for freight on the returned goods, as you sent these carriage forward; the cost of returning goods for exchange must, of course, be borne by the customer.

70

Will you please also let us know whether the replacement goods are to be sent at once, or whether we should include them in your monthly delivery. If we send specially, we shall have to charge the freight to you.

## VARYING THE TERMS OF PAYMENT

### [12] *Customer asks for open account terms*

Dear Sirs

Today we have arranged payment of your invoice no. 162 for goods received on 24 April. The material arrived in good condition and has now been sold.

As we have now done business with you for a year on the basis of payment on invoice, we would like to ask you to grant us open account terms, with quarterly settlement. Our two other main suppliers, Messrs. . . . and . . ., have recently agreed to supply us on these terms.

Yours faithfully

### [13] *Customer asks for monthly account terms*

We have now been doing business with you for nearly a year and are pleased to say that we are more than satisfied with the goods you have supplied.

In the coming year we will probably place regular orders with you and our present method of payment by letter of credit will become inconvenient. We would also find a short credit of advantage to our trading capacity.

We would therefore like you to supply us on monthly account terms, payment against statement within 30 days. You may refer to Messrs. . . . and Messrs. . . ., with whom we have credit accounts.

### [14] *Supplier agrees to account terms (Reply to letter no. 13)*

Many thanks for your letter of . . . in which you ask us to place you on monthly account terms.

We are pleased to hear that you propose to increase your business with us and are quite willing to comply with your request. The new arrangement will operate immediately.

We look forward to serving you and are delighted to hear that you are satisfied with the goods we have supplied.

## EXTENSION OF CREDIT

### [15] *Customer asks for time to pay*

Dear Sirs

Your quarterly statement reached us yesterday and has been found correct.

As you know, we have always settled your account promptly and regret very much that we now find it necessary to ask you for an extra few weeks in which to clear the current liability.[8]

Our difficulties are temporary and have been caused by the failure of the early fruit crop here, on which many of our customers are dependent. We are confident of being able to settle in full within 6–8 weeks.

We would appreciate it as a helpful gesture if you could grant us this concession.

Yours faithfully

## [16] *Supplier's reply to request for time to pay*

Dear Sirs

We have received your letter of . . . asking us to allow you 60 days in which to clear your current statement.

While appreciating your difficulties, we think it unreasonable to expect us to wait a further 2 months for payment for goods, many of which were supplied 2–3 months ago. However, we are taking your good record of settlement into consideration and are willing to help you as far as possible.

If you send us a remittance for half the amount of our statement we will draw on you at 60 d/s⁹ for the remaining half.

We hope this will be acceptable to you and wish you a speedy recovery from your difficulties.

Yours faithfully

## THE COLLECTION OF OVERDUE ACCOUNTS

There has probably never been a trading firm whose accounts department has not had to spend a considerable amount of time in trying to get customers to pay overdue accounts. In the home trade this is fairly common, but in foreign trade it is fortunately less frequent, as sellers usually insist on terms which secure payment, when dealing with customers they do not know. Accordingly the only risk comes from customers with open accounts, and as these are normally buyers with a proven reputation, this risk is small. However, it can and sometimes does happen that an account is not paid when due. A buyer may run into a period of bad trade and find himself temporarily short of money; he may have a complaint about the goods sent; he may refuse to accept a bill of exchange (*See Banking*); or delays and misunderstandings may be caused by customs regulations in his country. A wise customer will inform his supplier of any such situation and try to get some concession from him. If he does not, and an account becomes overdue, the seller has the task of asking for payment.

As in the home trade, it is usual to make the first request for payment brief and polite. After all, the matter may be an oversight, and the simple act of sending a copy of the account with a remark such as 'Overdue—please settle' or 'Kindly remit' may be all that is necessary. Alternatively, a cable or telex may be sent. This saves time, gives a sense of urgency to the matter, and has in many cases proved effective.

If, however, a firm decides to send a letter requesting payment, the style or tone of the letter will depend on the kind of customer for whom it is intended; how long overdue; whether customer has previously allowed accounts to become overdue; how valuable the business is, etc.

72

A first request will usually be friendly in tone, be accompanied by a copy of the account, and show neither annoyance nor any hint of doubt about the customer's intention to pay.

## Suggested opening lines for a first reminder

30. We have to draw your attention to our statement dated 10 July for the amount of £385, and to remind you that settlement was due by 31 July.
31. Will you please let us have your draft in settlement of our invoice no. 7933417 of 17 May.
32. We are sorry to have to inform you that we have not yet received a credit advice from our bank in connection with the consignment which was sent to you on 24 February (our invoice no. 682435).
33. We sent you our quarterly statement on 4 April, but since we have not received any advice of payment we are enclosing a copy of the statement and would be glad if you would kindly arrange early settlement.

## [17] A first reminder to a previously regular payer

Dear Sirs

As we have always received your payments punctually, we are puzzled to have had neither remittance nor report from you in connection with our current statement of 7 April.

We think you may not have received our letter containing the statement, as settlement is now 4 weeks overdue. We are accordingly enclosing a copy of the account to the amount of £. . . and you will no doubt give it your early attention.

Yours faithfully

## [18] A first reminder to a new credit account customer

Under our agreement, payment for individual orders sent to you is due 2 months from date of invoice.

The consignment of watch springs sent you by air freight on 15 June was invoiced to you on 16 June and payment was accordingly due on 16 August.

No doubt it is through an oversight on your part that settlement is now 3 weeks overdue and we look forward to receiving your remittance in the course of a few days.

May we ask you for prompt clearance of all invoiced accounts, as we can only supply at our agreed prices if this is done.

## [19] Customer makes part-payment after receiving a first reminder

Dear Sirs

We have received your letter of 15 August reminding us that your account was due for payment on 31 July. We intended to clear this account by the end of last month, but business has been slack in the fur trade, and our own customers have been very slow in clearing their accounts. This has, of course, resulted in a temporary liquidity problem for us.

Today we have sent you a cheque for £750, which we must ask you to accept on account. We will send you a further sum in a fortnight's time, and will clear the balance outstanding by the end of September.

We are very sorry to have to keep you waiting, but hope you will <u>realise</u> that we are doing everything we can under difficult circumstances.

Yours faithfully

If the seller does not receive a reply to his first request within a reasonable period, he will normally send a second and even a third letter before <u>taking action</u> through <u>legal</u> channels to obtain the money due to him. Just how many such letters should be sent and what tone to adopt in their phrasing will depend on individual circumstances. For the purposes of this chapter we will draw the line at three letters.

## *Here are some suggestions for a second reminder*

[20]

We regret very much that you have not replied to our letter of . . . asking you to clear the amount of £. . . outstanding against invoice no. 000. Kindly <u>inform us</u> if there are any reasonable grounds for your non-payment, or alternatively <u>advise</u> us of what arrangements you are making for settlement.

[21]

On 1 April we sent you our statement showing a balance due of £. . . This sum should have been paid by 30 April, but, receiving no remittance, we wrote to you again on 25 May, enclosing a copy of the statement. As we are still without any reply from you, we regret to say that we must hold your order no. 1111 until we have your payment or an explanation of your delay in replying to our letters.

[22]

No reply appears to have been received to our letter of . . . asking for clearance of the balance of your account. We are quite sure that you have some good reason for your failure to pay this sum within the agreed time, but regret very much that you have not informed us of it. Whatever the reason, however, we must remind you that our terms are 30 days net. We expect your reply by telex or cable.

[23]

Since sending you a reminder on 31 October, we have not pressed you for settlement of our September statement because on the whole your payments have been satisfactory since we granted you open account terms. Please do not make it necessary for us to <u>revise</u> our terms of business by <u>withholding</u> payment any longer. We look forward to receiving your immediate draft.

[24]

When we placed you on open account terms it was agreed between us that settlement would be made within 30 days of date of statement. Your payments have not always been made in accordance with our agreement and your present balance of £215.18 is now a month overdue. It is impossible for us <u>to continue supplying</u> you unless you meet your obligations promptly and we now have to ask you to confirm by cable that you have arranged for payment.

The third letter—which for our purposes is the *final demand*—has to show that the writer cannot and will not wait any longer for his money and that he now intends to take action to enforce payment. He may turn for assistance to a bank, a debt-collecting agency, a trade association, or a solicitor: it depends on the circumstances of the case in question.

*Here are some sentences which might be used in a final demand*

34. As we have received no replies to our letters of . . . and . . ., we have no option but to take immediate legal action to recover the amount due to us unless your payment is received within 7 days.
35. We are sorry to have to inform you that as we cannot get any satisfactory reply from you regarding settlement of our account we shall have to refer the matter to the . . . Trade Association in your town, unless we receive some news from you within 3 days.
36. It is impossible to keep this account open any longer and we are taking measures to obtain payment through legal channels.
37. We have given you every opportunity of discharging your debt but have had no evidence of your willingness to honour your obligations. We are therefore instructing our solicitors to take the necessary action to enforce payment.

[25]

Dear Sirs

Our letters KP/1–KP/2 of . . .

All our attempts to induce you to clear your indebtedness to us have been ignored, and we are quite unable to understand why you have not even replied to our letters.

We think we have shown reasonable patience and consideration, but we can do so no longer and must now reluctantly take steps to obtain payment at law.

As you must yourselves appreciate, your own credit and reputation are certain to suffer by our action, but we regret that there is no alternative. If, however, you make an immediate payment to . . . Bank of the full amount due, we will suspend action against you.

Yours faithfully

# MISCELLANEOUS PHRASES AND SENTENCES ON ACCOUNTING

## *Debit, credit, balance*

38. Please credit us with this amount.
39. Kindly place these funds to the credit of our account.
40. Your account is £. . . in credit.
41. There is now a debit balance of £. . .
42. This payment balances our account to date.
43. There is an outstanding balance of £. . .
44. We are opening a credit of £. . . in your favour.
45. There is a balance of $. . . to your credit.
46. Please apply these funds to clear our account, and carry the balance forward to 19. . .

75

## Charge, charges

47. You may charge this item to us. *je mag het ons aanrekenen*
48. We are charging your account with the balance. *We voegen het saldo bij uw rekening*
49. Our charge for this service is . . . *opgelopen kosten*
50. This item represents charges for costs incurred.
51. Transport and dock charges are included. *inbegrepen*
52. We make no charge for this item. *We rekenen dit niet aan*
53. You sent us three cases but charged for four.
54. There is no charge for cardboard cartons.
55. Any incidental costs are chargeable to us. *komen voor onze rekening*
56. We are sure that this is an overcharge. *dat u teveel hebt aangerekend*
57. We regret having undercharged for item XX.
58. This payment discharges our liability. *voldoet onze schuld.*

## Enter, entries  *voegen bij (boeken)*  *past*

59. Please enter this item in your records.
60. After entering these credits we find our figures agree with yours.
61. After making these entries we can confirm your total.
62. Kindly make similar entries in your books.
63. On checking your statement we find that you have missed a credit entry for £. . . on 3 Jan. *credit post*

Note: In the above examples the words *debit, credit,* and *charge* can be used both as nouns and verbs. The same is possible with *invoice*.

## Books, audit  *accountance onderzoek*

64. Our books are due for audit.
65. These are the auditor's figures. *cijfers vd accountant*
66. Please clear this amount at once . . .
67. . . . as our books have to be balanced on 31 December.
68. . . . as we close our books on . . .
69. . . . as we wish to close our books.
70. We shall audit the accounts on . . . *de rekeningen nazien*
71. The annual audit will be made on . . . *nazicht*

*Note* the following verbs used in book-keeping:  *overeenkomen*
*adjust ( = put right), correct, rectify; agree, correspond, concur ( = be in agreement); calculate, estimate, figure ( = to work out), reckon; check ( = examine) (do not use 'control'); extend.*

*Also* note these arithmetical verbs:  *optellen*
*add; subtract (or deduct); multiply; divide*  *aftrekken*  *delen*
*Note* the following titles:  *hulp-boekhouder*
*accountant: auditor; book-keeper; cashier; ledger-clerk*


## OPENING A NEW ACCOUNT—CREDIT STATUS

Any buyer who finds he is likely to make regular purchases from a particular seller will almost certainly ask for open account terms, i.e. he wishes to be supplied without payment for each order separately at time

76

of delivery. He may want to pay monthly or quarterly (i.e. 3-monthly). In other words, he wants *credit* from his supplier just as his own customers will probably want credit from him. Credit is the life-blood of trade. Modern commerce has been built up on it and it has in recent years penetrated to the retail buyer to such an extent that today many people spend half their income on credit buying, and large credit finance companies have sprung up to finance this kind of spending.

In international trade, credit is of even greater importance than in the home trade, partly because of the timelag between the placing of the order and delivery of the goods. It is not only buyers who intend to place regular orders who will want credit terms, but also buyers who may want to place a single—but very large—order. Very often the banks will cover the credits required, and this is dealt with in Chapter 9. In the present chapter we shall deal only with credit given by the seller himself.

Let us suppose a seller has received a request for account terms. The seller needs to know immediately what kind of reputation the buyer has, the approximate size of his business, how he pays his accounts and even something about his trade activities, before the seller can calculate how much credit he can grant. This level of credit is called *credit standing* or *credit status*.

The seller can obtain information from (*a*) references given by the buyer, (*b*) his bank, (*c*) various trade associations and (*d*) enquiry agencies.

In writing letters asking for information of this kind, the writer must remember that the whole matter is *confidential* and that in the cases of (*b*) and (*c*), the giving of information is a favour on the part of the givers. Letters should therefore be polite and appreciative and should give assurance of confidential treatment.

[26] *Seller's enquiry to reference given by buyers*

CONFIDENTIAL

Dear Sirs

We have had a request from Messrs. J. L. Dyer & Co. of Port Elizabeth S.A. for supplies of our products on open account terms. They have given your name as a reference, saying they have done business with you for the past 5 years.

We would appreciate it as a very great favour if you would kindly let us know in confidence whether you have found Messrs. Dyer & Co. reliable in their dealings and prompt in settling their accounts. As we understand that their requirements may be to the amount of £1,000 monthly, we should be grateful to you for an opinion on their ability to meet[10] a liability of this size.

Any other information which you could supply would be very welcome, and would of course be treated as strictly confidential.

Yours faithfully

## [27] *Seller's letter to trade association*

Dear Sirs

We have been referred to you for information on their credit standing by Messrs. D. Lyle & Co. who have asked us to supply goods to the value of £750 against their first order.

We should be very grateful to you for any information you can give us about their activities and the scope of their transactions, as we hear that they may place further and larger orders. In particular we should like to know whether you think we should be taking a fair risk in granting a £750 credit in respect of this first order, and up to what amount you think we could go with safety in the future.

We thank you for your courtesy and assure you of strict confidence.

Yours faithfully

(Large firms often print a special form setting out questions which the giver of information is asked to answer. This is an excellent method, for it saves the information-giver's time and is therefore fairly sure of a prompt response.)

## [28] *Seller's letter to his bank manager, asking for information*

The Manager
North-Eastern Bank Ltd.
Hadley St.
Newcastle ND2 7GF

Dear Sir

I am thinking of granting credit to Messrs. . . . of . . ., of whom I have only slight knowledge gained during a few months of trading on a cash basis.

If you can find out anything about their financial and credit standing, I shall be very grateful to you. They give me only their bankers, The . . . Bank Ltd. of . . ., as a reference, and they estimate their monthly orders at about £500.

I hope that you will be able to assist me.

Yours faithfully

## *Some phrases for use in letters enquiring about a customer's credit status*

72. Your name was given us by . . .
73. We are indebted to Messrs. . . . for your name.
74. Messrs. . . . have referred us to you for information concerning . . .
75. We have been asked to give credit of . . .
76. The firm whose name is written on the attached slip . . .
77. (Can you please) (Will you kindly) give us information regarding . . .
78. . . . their credit status.
79. . . . their activities and financial standing.
80. . . . their reputation and creditworthiness.
81. . . . their ability to meet a credit of . . .
82. Do you think they should be good for £. . . ?
83. Would you consider a credit of £. . . a reasonable risk?
84. Have you any reason to doubt their creditworthiness?

78

85. Are they reputed to meet their liabilities promptly? *do they have the reputation of*
86. As far as you know, is their business financially sound? *financial ground*
87. Should we be safe in granting them a credit of £. . . ?
88. We should also welcome information regarding . . .
89. Any other information you may be able to pass on to us will be treated as confidential.
90. You can, of course, rely on us to act discreetly.
91. We realise that what you may be able to tell us is without responsibility.
92. We enclose a (stamped addressed envelope) (postal reply coupon) for your reply, and thank you in anticipation. *antwoordcoupon*
93. We would be very grateful to you for an answer, and enclose a postal reply coupon.
94. If we can at any time render you a similar service, we shall be glad to do so.
95. We thank you in anticipation of your reply . . .
96. We thank you very much for your assistance.

Letters asking for information, such as we have just studied, are part of recognised business procedure. The receivers of these letters regard it as a duty to answer them honestly, although there is no necessity for them to do so. They act on the fairly certain assumption that they themselves will one day need assistance of the same kind.

Replies to these enquiries should therefore be helpful but brief. It is not necessary to write a history of the firm in question, but enough should be said to give the enquirer a fair basis for reaching a decision. Banks usually answer very briefly indeed, private firms somewhat more fully, while enquiry agencies usually go into much more detail.

One must be very careful when giving negative or unfavourable information. To write a letter saying that someone is unreliable can lead to trouble in almost any country, and in Great Britain it might easily be libel. *smaad* A safe course in such cases is to say that you cannot give any favourable information, and let the enquirer draw his own conclusions.

[29] *Favourable reply to letter no. 26*

STRICTLY CONFIDENTIAL

Dear Sirs

Replying to your letter of . . . under ref. no. AB/A we can give you the following information.

The firm you mention are well-known in local business circles and appear to have a good reputation. They have been established for over 10 years, to our knowledge, and conduct a fairly extensive import trade in our line.

We have been doing business with them for just over 5 years on quarterly account terms and can say that their obligations to us have been punctually met[11] at all times. Although their credit with us has never reached the level mentioned in your letter we would have no hesitation in granting them this amount, if asked.

This information is given without responsibility,[12] of course.

Yours faithfully

79

## [30] *Favourable reply to letter no. 27*

Dear Sirs

We can supply the following facts regarding the firm mentioned in your enquiry of 3 November.

Established in 1935 as import/export dealers, they now have a sound business with a high turnover. They own good premises and have an office staff of 30.

Local enquiries reveal that their annual purchases exceed £10,000. Their directors are well-known locally and well thought of.

Our opinion is that the credit you name could safely be granted: the figure given above in respect of other credit transactions may act as a guide to you in fixing your credit level.

We hope this information will be of assistance to you.

Yours faithfully

## [31] *Favourable reply from a bank to letter no. 28*

Dear Sirs

With reference to your enquiry of . . . concerning the firm named on the enclosed slip, we can advise you that they are old established dealers of the highest repute and standing, and are considered safe for the credit you mention.

This information is for your own use only and is given without responsibility.[12]

Yours faithfully

## [32] *Unfavourable reply from a bank to letter no. 28*

Dear Sirs

Replying to your enquiry DD/CC of . . . we regret to say that we cannot give information in this case. We would advise you to act with caution.

Yours faithfully

## [33] *Unfavourable reply from enquiry agency*

Dear Sirs

We have completed our enquiries concerning the firm mentioned in your letter of . . . and must advise you to consider carefully the credit you give in this case.

In the past 2 years this company has been the defendant in 2 court cases involving claims for non-payment of sums due, although payment was subsequently made in each instance.

Overbuying[13] would appear to be a fault in this firm, whose registered capital (1974) was £750. As a result, most of their suppliers give them very short credit or supply only on a cash basis.

This information is strictly confidential and is given without responsibility on our part.

Yours faithfully

## [34] *Unfavourable reply from business reference*

Dear Sirs

We regret we are unable to help you very much with regard to the firm mentioned in your letter of . . .

It is true that we did business with them during the period 1974–75, but the amount involved was not large and accounts were not always satisfactorily kept.[14]

This is, of course, in strict confidence.

Yours faithfully

## Phrases and sentences used when answering credit enquiries

97. The firm (you name) (named in your letter) (mentioned) . . .
98. . . . are reputed to be sound.
99. . . . have a high standing.
100. . . . enjoy the respect and confidence of . . .
101. . . . have a sound and prosperous business.
102. . . . are considered worthy of credit.
103. . . . have an excellent record.
104. Messrs. XXX . . .
105. . . . have done business with us for . . . years.
106. . . . are good customers of ours.
107. . . . have been known to us for . . . years.
108. . . . are a well established and reliable firm.
109. . . . have an old established connection . . .
110. . . . are people of integrity.
111. We think a credit of £500 a fair risk.
112. A credit of £1,000 would be justified.
113. We are of the opinion that you would run no undue risk in granting them quarterly account terms.
114. We should not hesitate to allow them the credit asked.
115. Monthly terms with a credit limit of £500 would appear to be reasonable.
116. They should be safe for almost any amount.
117. We advise caution in granting credit terms.
118. In view of their position, credit of £. . . would be risky.
119. Credit should be restricted to one month.
120. We advise against exceeding a credit of £200.
121. A credit of £1,000 would be a great risk.
122. Long credit would involve you in serious risk.
123. They are a firm of good repute and have large financial reserves.
124. Their financial standing is very strong.
125. They have the capital to back this expansion.
126. Their credit status is very high.
127. They are known to be heavily committed and have overrun their reserves. Caution is advisable.
128. They are being pressed by several creditors and their position is precarious.
129. Their reputation is good, but they appear to have over-traded recently.
130. They suffered heavy loss in the . . . bankruptcy case and recovery is uncertain.
131. They are inexperienced in this business and extreme caution is advised in granting credit.
132. We would rather not express an opinion of this firm.
133. We are unable to recommend them.
134. Our experience of this firm does not warrant our giving you a favourable report.
135. We do not know enough about them to give satisfactory answers to your questions.
136. They are slow to settle their accounts.
137. They often defer payment of their accounts until a second reminder is sent to them.
138. Their record does not give grounds for confidence.

81

*Explanation of reference numbers in letters 1–34*

[1] *discrepancy*: Error; disagreement.

[2] *carriage*: Freight; cost of transport.

[3] *warrant*: Justify; entitle us to.

[4] *to query*: To question; raise a question.

[5] *to waive*: To cancel; overlook.

[6] *clerical error*: Office error.

[7] *outstanding*: Unpaid.

[8] *current liability*: Present debt; last account.

[9] *60 d/s*: 60 days after sight.

[10] *meet*: Pay.

[11] *punctually met*: Paid when due.

[12] *without responsibility*: No responsibility can be accepted.

[13] *overbuying*: Buying more than they can pay for.

[14] *kept*: (In this case) paid promptly.

## EXERCISES

1. Send a short letter for an export firm to a foreign customer, enclosing quarterly statement.

2. Send an order for goods your firm requires from a foreign supplier and ask for pro-forma invoice.

3. A customer of your firm left a balance of £50 on his last payment. Send a new monthly statement and ask for clearance.

4. Send an order for textiles to a British manufacturer with whom you have not yet done business and say how you propose to pay.

5. Your firm, an export dealer, receives an order from a new customer who does not say how he proposes to pay for the goods. Write a suitable reply.

6. Your firm has received a quarterly statement containing an item of which you have no record. Write a letter asking for an explanation.

7. Write a letter in which you ask your suppliers for an extra $2\frac{1}{2}\%$ discount on an order for 10,000 tins of meat extract. Write also the supplier's letter (*a*) granting, and (*b*) refusing this request.

8. Because of temporary financial difficulties you are unable to settle the account of one of your suppliers. Write asking for a 2-months' extension of credit. Write also the supplier's reply.

9. Your firm has a foreign customer whose business they value highly: the customer usually settles his account by banker's draft, but has failed to pay the latest account and has not given your firm any explanation; payment is now 6 weeks overdue. Write a tactful letter.

10. Send a suitable letter to an overseas buyer of your firm's products, in which you express your firm's total dissatisfaction with the manner in

which he is settling his accounts. Earlier letters have been ignored by the buyer.

11. You have been asked by an export firm in your country to give a reference for a foreign buyer with whom you are doing business. You are not completely satisfied with this buyer's account. Answer the enquiry.

12. Write a letter for your firm, an importer of glass and chinaware, to a foreign manufacturer from whom you wish to buy on quarterly account terms. Give details of your firm and your requirements, and offer references.

# 8 | Shipping and forwarding

Being an island, Great Britain is more dependent than are most countries on transport by sea. Although air transport is increasing and is undoubtedly the best method for carrying certain types of goods, its limitations are obvious.

Large amounts of merchandise are transported to the Continent by rail and lorry. There are special ferries which can carry a whole train or several loaded lorries, so that cargo does not have to be loaded, unloaded and reloaded at ports. Special wagons, both open and closed, are used on train-ferry services, and these include refrigerated wagons for perishable goods and tanks for liquids being transported in bulk.

*A cross-Channel Ferry Train*

In recent years this type of transport has greatly encouraged the use of containers, which are mentioned in Chapter 6. Container services provide speedy, safe, and relatively inexpensive door-to-door deliveries, and are becoming more and more popular with exporters and importers alike.

Transport by ferry is possible only between Britain and certain other European countries, so most goods, unless they are light enough to be carried economically by air, have to go by ship.

Carriage by sea can be a complicated business, since the exporter and the importer both have to observe a variety of rules and regulations which have been made over the years. These involve a great deal of paperwork which can be studied in detail in any of the available books on modern commercial practice: this chapter will explain only what it is necessary to mention in correspondence.

A lot of the letter writing concerning transport is between firms in the same country: for example, sellers make arrangements with forwarding agents or shipowners, while buyers frequently have to contact agents or carriers in their own country when goods are to be collected from a harbour, airport or railway station.

The seller or buyer—according to which party is responsible under the terms of payment for transport arrangements—has to know how much it will cost to have his goods delivered. If he is concerned with regular shipments between two specific ports, he will know the normal freight rates and will be kept informed of changes, but in other cases he will have to make enquiries, as in letters 1 and 2:

[1]

Dear Sirs

Please quote us your freight rate for *cased cycles* for shipment from London to Valetta, and let us know when you will be sailing to Malta during the next three months.

Yours faithfully

[2]

Dear Sirs

We are about to make up an order for a customer in Beirut for 3 cases textile machinery parts, and in accordance with the terms of the letter of credit the consignment has to be shipped by 15 January at the latest.

Please inform us whether your *S.S. Morning Star* will be able to meet our requirements, and kindly quote us a rate for the voyage.

We are looking forward to hearing from you.

Yours faithfully

Page 86 shows a sailing card issued by a shipping line, giving particulars of loading and sailing dates of a cargo vessel sailing between Britain and South America. When sailings are infrequent, space has to be reserved in advance.

**P.S.N.C.**
**ROYAL MAIL LINES**
Members of the
Furness Withy Group

# THE PACIFIC STEAM NAVIGATION CO.

Wheelwright House,
157 Regent Road,
Liverpool L5 9YF

Tel. 051-922 7222
Telex 629230/629441
Telegrams 'PACIFIC'

**Loading Berth: South Vittoria Dock, Birkenhead**

OPERATIONAL SCHEDULE

## Container / Break Bulk Service

U.K./ISLANDS/JAMAICA/CARTAGENA/CRISTOBAL/WEST COAST SOUTH AMERICA/U.K. SERVICE

| VESSEL | RECEIVING DATES | SAILS/SAILED LIVERPOOL | OUTWARD (ARRIVES) | | | | | | | | | | | | | | HOMEWARD (ARRIVES) | | | | | |
|---|---|---|---|---|---|---|---|---|---|---|---|---|---|---|---|---|---|---|---|---|---|---|
| | | | BERMUDA | FREEPORT | NASSAU | KINGSTON | CARTAGENA | CRISTOBAL | BUENAVENTURA | GUAYAQUIL | CALLAO | MATARANI | ARICA | ANTOFAGASTA | VALPARAISO | SAN ANTONIO | ANTOFAGASTA | ILO | CALLAO | CRISTOBAL | KINGSTON | U.K. (AVONMOUTH) |
| ORBITA 19 | | 9 AUG | 17 AUG | 20 AUG | 21 AUG | 24 AUG | – | 27 AUG | – | 31 AUG | 3 SEP | 6 SEP | 8 SEP | 9 SEP | 12 SEP | 14 SEP | 16 SEP | 19 SEP | 21 SEP | 25 SEP | – | 9 OCT |
| OROYA 02 | | 30 AUG | 7 SEP | – | 10 SEP | 13 SEP | 15 SEP | 18 SEP | 21 SEP | 26 SEP | 29 SEP | 3 OCT | 6 OCT | 7 OCT | 9 OCT | 13 OCT | 15 OCT | 18 OCT | 20 OCT | 24 OCT | 27 OCT | 7 NOV |
| ORTEGA 19 | 29 AUG - 7 SEP | 13 SEP | 21 SEP | 24 SEP | 25 SEP | 28 SEP | – | 1 OCT | 4 OCT | 9 OCT | 12 OCT | 16 OCT | 19 OCT | 20 OCT | 22 OCT | 25 OCT | 27 OCT | 29 OCT | 31 OCT | 4 NOV | 7 NOV | 18 NOV |
| ORDUNA 19 | 18 - 29 SEP | 4 OCT | 12 OCT | – | 15 OCT | 18 OCT | 21 OCT | 24 OCT | – | 29 OCT | 2 NOV | 6 NOV | 9 NOV | 10 NOV | 13 NOV | 16 NOV | 19 NOV | 21 NOV | 23 NOV | 27 NOV | 30 NOV | 10 DEC |
| ORBITA 20 | 11 - 26 OCT | 31 OCT | 7 NOV | 10 NOV | 11 NOV | 14 NOV | – | 17 NOV | 20 NOV | 25 NOV | 28 NOV | 2 DEC | 5 DEC | 6 DEC | 9 DEC | 12 DEC | 15 DEC | 17 DEC | 19 DEC | 23 DEC | 26 DEC | 6 JAN |
| OROPESA 01 (Maiden Voyage) | 1 - 10 NOV | 15 NOV | 23 NOV | – | 26 NOV | 29 NOV | 2 DEC | 5 DEC | – | 9 DEC | 12 DEC | 16 DEC | 19 DEC | 20 DEC | 23 DEC | 26 DEC | 29 DEC | 31 DEC | 2 JAN | 6 JAN | 9 JAN | 20 JAN |
| OROYA 03 | 22 NOV - 1 DEC | 6 DEC | 13 DEC | 16 DEC | 17 DEC | 20 DEC | – | 23 DEC | 26 DEC | 31 DEC | 3 JAN | 7 JAN | 10 JAN | 11 JAN | 14 JAN | 17 JAN | 20 JAN | 22 JAN | 24 JAN | 28 JAN | 31 JAN | 11 FEB |

**Cargo Space (Outward)**
Please contact our Bookings Section Tel. 051-922 7222 or our Agents.

**Vehicle Appointments System**
An appointments scheme is in operation at our loading berth, South Vittoria Dock, Birkenhead. Tel. 051-653 7055.

**London Terminal**
L.C.L. Cargo for Bermuda – Nassau – Kingston – Cristobal (Also Colon and Panama) received at Comclear Terminal, Royal Victoria Dock E.16, prior booking required with Brantford International Ltd., Barking, Tel. 01-594 7181

**Glasgow Terminal**
L.C.L. Cargo for Kingston & Cristobal (incl. Colon and Panama) received at Coatbridge Container Base (0236-24331). Prior booking required with Furness & Salvesen (Agencies) Ltd. Glasgow. Tel. 041-248 3631.

**Cargo Space (Homeward)**
Enquiries to:–
P.S.N.C.
Agustinas 1066/1070 P.O. Box 4087, Santiago, Chile. Telex 40484-40590-354

OR

P.S.N.C. Nicolas De Pierola 1002/1006 P.O. Box 1138, Lima, Peru Telex 25211

### STOP PRESS

WE WOULD DRAW YOUR PARTICULAR ATTENTION TO OUR CHANGE OF BERTH TO:- VITTORIA DOCK, BIRKENHEAD.

THIS OFFERS GREATLY IMPROVED FACILITIES INCLUDING CLOSE ACCESS TO M53 MOTORWAY, RAIL CONNECTION AND LARGE VEHICLE PARKING AREAS.

LIVERPOOL DATED BILLS OF LADING WILL BE ISSUED.

The following additional ports are served subject to inducement:

MANTA
LA LIBERTAD
PAITA
PIMENTEL
ETEN
CHIMBOTE
SALAVERRY
IQUIQUE
COQUIMBO
TALCAHUANO
SAN VICENTE

THE DATES AND PORTS OF LOADING SHOWN ABOVE ARE BASED ON THE LATEST INFORMATION AVAILABLE AND SHOULD BE REGARDED AS INDICATIONS ONLY AND NOT AS FIXED SCHEDULES

LIVERPOOL. 29th. AUGUST 1978                    ROUTE MANAGEMENT DIVISION No 35

## [3] *Reply from shipowners to letter no. 1*

Dear Sirs

We have received your enquiry of 4 December, and can inform you that our current freight rate for cased cycles, London–Valetta, is £. . . per metric tonne or 10 cubic metres, at steamer's option.[1]

We sail once a week, and as Malta is our first port of call the voyage takes about six days. We enclose our sailing card for *M.V. Morecombe*, which loads at the West India Docks, and our shipping instructions form. We would appreciate it if you would kindly complete and return the latter as soon as possible.

Yours faithfully

## [4] *Reply from agents to letter no. 2*

Dear Sirs

In reply to your letter of 12 December, we are pleased to inform you that the *S.S. Morning Star* of the Blue Crescent Line will be receiving cargo from 12 to 18 January inclusive, and is expected to commence loading[2] on 14th. We see no reason why your goods should not be on board by this date, but suggest that the three cases should be delivered to the ship on the opening date.

Details of the Blue Crescent Line's rates are enclosed.

We look forward to assisting you.

Yours faithfully

Enclosure

If the consignor finds the rates acceptable, he will send an *advice note* to the shipowners or agents.

## [5] *Shipping instructions sent to shipping company*

Dear Sirs

Thank you for your letter of 5 December. We have noted that your *M.V. Morecombe* is receiving cargo for Malta on the 10th of this month, and are making arrangements for our cycles to be delivered to the West India Docks.

We are enclosing your shipping instructions form, duly completed.

Yours faithfully

When arrangements have been made for shipping the goods, the senders will write to the buyers to inform them that the merchandise is on the way. This communication is known as an *advice of despatch*, and normally the information is typed on a printed form. Sometimes, however, a letter is written instead, and occasionally a form is sent together with a covering note.

*[6] Supplier informs customer that order has been despatched*

---

# SPEEDSURE CYCLES  NEASDEN
NW10 0DD

13 December 1977

Dear Sirs

YOUR ORDER NO. 2231/c OF 30 NOVEMBER 1977

We are pleased to inform you that the cycles ordered under the above number
have been despatched as arranged.

The cycles are packed in 6 cases, 2 to a case.  The cases are marked FBC
in square, MALTA, and are numbered 1-6.

The consignment is arriving at Malta on 24 December, on the m.v. Morecombe,
which sailed from London yesterday.

Clean, shipped on board Bs/L in complete set, together with a commercial
invoice and insurance certificate, both in triplicate, have been handed to
Barclays Bank, Lombard St, EC4, together with our sight draft for £385,
in accordance with the terms of the letter of credit opened with them.
Barclays Bank have paid the sum.

We are sure you will be more than satisfied with the cycles, and look
forward to hearing from you again.

Yours faithfully

---

*Notes on letter no. 6*

The *bill of lading* (generally abbreviated in correspondence to B/L) is a
very important shipping document. Firstly, it is a *receipt* from the shipowners, giving details of the shipment in question and the conditions
under which they accept it: so it is evidence of a *contract*. Secondly, the
B/L is the *legal title* to the consignment, and can be used to transfer the
right of ownership to the goods.

The B/L is known as *shipped*, or *shipped on board*, when the goods
have been loaded onto the vessel named on it. Shipped bills are usually
required in transactions involving payment through a bank. The term
*clean B/L* means that the shipowners have examined the cargo and
accepted it for delivery in 'the like good order and condition'. If the goods
do not correspond to the description of them on the bill, it is known as
*dirty, unclean, foul*, or *claused* (because a clause has been added to it by
the shipowners, specifying the discrepancy).

The *invoice* is the account of what the buyers have purchased and what they have to pay. The final account, made out when the goods have been despatched, is usually called the *commercial invoice*. When there is no bill of lading, as in transport by road or rail, the invoice is used when payment is made through a bank.

Letter no. 6 is concerned with a CIF contract, whereby the senders arrange to transport the consignment to the docks, have it loaded, and pay the freight to the port of destination. The senders also insure the goods until they arrive at the port in the buyers' country. The costs of all these functions are included in the quotation made by the sellers.

Banks play a very important part in carrying through transactions, and their role in international trade is dealt with in Chapter 9.

## AIR TRANSPORT

The document used for transport by air is called an *air waybill*. It is like a B/L in some ways, but is *not* a document of title: in other words, it cannot be used to pass on the right of ownership to the goods. Airlines themselves complete the waybills on the basis of information provided by consignors. An example of a British Airways waybill is given on page 90.

In the example letters given so far we have dealt with shipment by sea. In the following lists there are phrases and sentences which can be used in correspondence relating to other methods of transport.

## GENERAL TRANSPORT

*Enquiries for freight rates and loading dates*

1. Please quote your inclusive rates on the following (cargo) (consignment).
2. Please let us know the present freight rates for . . .
3. Please advise us of the current rates of freight on . . .
4. We shall be glad to know time of transit and frequency of sailings, and whether cargo space must be reserved; if so, please send us the necessary application forms.
5. Please advise us of the loading dates.
6. Please let us know on which day the ship closes for cargo.[3]
7. We shall be glad to know (your lowest rates for large shipments) (your groupage rates[4] for small consignments).
8. We would be grateful if you would send us your current tariffs.
9. We have received an urgent order for the shipment of machines and spare parts, from Birmingham to Paris, and would appreciate an all-in rate including collection from works, Birmingham, and delivery to station, Paris.
10. Please let us know the difference in cost between transport by train-ferry via Dover/Dunkerque and road-ship-road via Newhaven/Dieppe. If there is any likelihood of delay we would prefer to have goods carried by road and ship, and not depend on the railway.
11. We are prepared to pay the G.V.[5] rate by train-ferry if absolutely necessary, to avoid delay.
12. F.O.B. charges are to our a/c; all other charges (will be paid by the consignee) (are to be debited to the consignee).

| SHIPPER | | FOR CARRIER'S USE ONLY<br>**AWB No.** |
|---|---|---|

**SHIPPER**

TELEPHONE No.

**CONSIGNEE**

# British airways cargo

## Instructions for Dispatch of Goods

**COMMON MARKET COUNTRIES**

| Goods destined to Countries within the E.E.C. | Yes |
|---|---|
| Do you require British Airways to raise Community Transit documents for you (T2L's)? | No |

To BRITISH AIRWAYS

Please dispatch the undermentioned goods in accordance with instructions contained herein:—

| REQUESTED ROUTING | BOOKING REFERENCE (if any) |
|---|---|
| AIRPORT OF DEPARTURE | |
| AIRPORT OF DESTINATION | |

| MARKS AND NUMBERS | NUMBERS AND KIND OF PACKAGES | DESCRIPTION OF GOODS | GROSS WEIGHT | DIMENSIONS |
|---|---|---|---|---|
| | | | | |

**FREIGHT CHARGES**
(Mark one to apply)
☐ PREPAID
☐ COLLECT (If Service Available)

**OTHER CHARGES At Origin**
(Mark one to apply)
☐ PREPAID
☐ COLLECT (If Service Available)

### DECLARED VALUE

| For Carriage | For Customs |
|---|---|

**HANDLING INFORMATION AND REMARKS**

### RESTRICTED ARTICLES

Goods having corrosive, explosive, flammable, poisonous or other hazardous characteristics must be accompanied by a "Shipper's Certification For Restricted Articles" completed in duplicate. Supplies of this Certificate may be obtained from the cargo offices of British Airways.

### The Sender Hereby:

(i)     expressly declares that the particulars furnished by him or his agent and contained herein are correct and that he is aware of and accepts the CONDITIONS OF CARRIAGE FOR CARGO which can be inspected at the carrier's Booking Office and which will be incorporated in the Consignment Note(s).

(ii)     authorises and requests that British Airways complete Consignment Notes and other Documents in connection with dispatch, carriage and delivery of the goods as agents for and on behalf of the sender as provided by the (CONDITIONS OF CARRIAGE FOR CARGO) Art. 3, Para. 3.

| SIGNATURE OF SHIPPER OR HIS AGENT | DATE |
|---|---|

T1396

90

13. According to the terms of the contract the shipment is to be effected by 10 June and we must have the Bs/L by the 15th at the latest.
14. Shipped, clean Bs/L, in a set of 3, are to be made out 'to order', and are required by 25 October for delivery to the . . . Bank, under the terms of a letter of credit.
15. In view of the fragile nature of the goods we require them to be forwarded by air, and we would therefore be glad to know the lowest rates.

## Replies to enquiries for freight rates

16. In reply to your letter of 10 August, the rates we can quote you are as follows:
17. Weekly sailings are available from . . . to . . . every Wednesday.
18. Our rates are subject to alteration without previous notice, except in the case of special contract.
19. We can offer you a substantial rebate for regular shipments.
20. We can ship your consignment by (M.V.) (S.S.) . . . closing for cargo on 18 August.
21. The closing date for cargo by S.S. Primavera is . . .
22. The M.V. Mercury will be loading cargo from . . . to . . .
23. We thank you for your enquiry of 8 November and attach our quotation for the packing as required. As you know, freight will depend on the size and weight of the (cases) (packages).
24. We enclose our shipping instructions form and will be glad if you will fill this in and return it to us, together with a copy of the invoice, for customs clearance abroad; we will then undertake all formalities on your behalf, in accordance with our usual conditions.

## Sellers' or agents' enquiry for shipping instructions

25. The goods of your order no. . . . are packed and ready for despatch, and we would be pleased if you would fill up, sign and return the attached instructions form as soon as possible.
26. Please let us know whether you wish to have the goods sent by the train-ferry or by ship to Rouen and thence by lighter. The Paris/London Line will have a vessel sailing from the Port of London on . . .

## Shipping instructions sent

27. Will you please collect from the address below (above) and arrange suitable land transport to London, for a consignment by a steamer of the . . . Line.
28. Instructions have been given to the manufacturers to forward to you by rail, carriage paid, the following consignment:
29. We enclose commercial invoice in triplicate; also certificate of origin.
30. We require 2 sets of shipped, clean Bs/L, consigned to your Paris (branch) (agents).
31. The consignees hold import licence no. . . .
32. We have consigned to the Superintendent, Nine Elms Goods Station, London, to your order, by lorry (van), the following goods:
33. We thank you for your letter of October 20th and we now return your shipping instructions form duly completed, with 2 copies of commercial invoice attached. The certificate of origin is printed on the back of the invoice and has been filled in.
34. The tractors are to be delivered F.A.S. by lighter to S.S. Orient, Port of London.
35. The goods are to be shipped by the first available vessel to Antwerp for transhipment to Rhine lighters, and we shall be glad if you will make the necessary arrangements for this on a through bill of lading.
36. As the cargo is to be transhipped at . . . we shall require through Bs/L.
37. To avoid undue risk of breakage we should like to have the carboys sent by train-ferry.
38. We would advise shipping by special tank.

b

39. The four casks of . . . have been despatched by lorry, consigned to the Superintendent, Colonial Wharf, Wapping, London, E., to your order.
40. All charges are payable by us and the Bs/L are to be marked 'freight prepaid'.

## Shipping agents acknowledge shipping instructions

41. Your instructions have been noted and we will collect the consignment for despatch by the next available opportunity overland.
42. We thank you for your letter enclosing routing order,⁶ which we are submitting to the suppliers today.
43. A waybill, giving full particulars, will be sent to you as soon as the consignment is ready for despatch by British Airways.
44. We have delivered to . . ., agents for the . . . Line, the goods of your order no. . . ., according to the enclosed copy invoice. We are advised that a vessel will sail on Wednesday so that the consignment should reach you within a week from that day.

## [7] Agents inform consignee of arrival of ship and goods

As brokers for the Jacobsdattir Line, we are writing to inform you that the following goods are arriving for your account on the M.V. Montefiore, due at Liverpool on 6 February.

In order to have the consignment cleared at Customs, we would be obliged if you would let us have the bill of lading, duly endorsed, together with a letter to H.M. Customs authorising us to act on your behalf.

At the same time please let us have the address to which you would like us to deliver the cases.

## [8]

We have received your letter of 1 February and the bill of lading relating to the consignment on board the M.V. Montefiore, which is due on 6 February.

When the goods arrive we will do what is necessary to have them dealt with promptly and delivered to your Manchester premises.

We note that the letter addressed to H.M. Customs is to follow.

## Shipping and forwarding agents and export packers offer their services

45. We collect your goods to be packed, by any method required for transport by sea, air, rail or road. We arrange shipments to any part of the world and will undertake all formalities on your behalf, clearing all documents and obtaining bills of lading.
46. We have connections throughout the world and as a result of our wide experience we can advise you on suitable packing and method of transport for any country to which you wish to export.
47. We can quote you for any type of packing—fragile articles or heavy machinery.
48. The enclosed folder will show you the type of precision packing in which we specialise.
49. Our plant is equipped to handle any type of bulky product, and we provide all the necessary internal fitments, bracing members and cushioning to avoid shock.
50. You can save both time and money by letting us handle all shipping and Customs formalities for you.
51. Our enclosed brochure will give you details of the varied services we can render and we are able to offer special reductions for large shipments. On the other hand we can quote very favourable groupage rates.

# TRANSHIPMENT

## [9] *Letter to a forwarding agency concerning a transhipment*

Messrs. Paulino of Milan have informed us that you are their correspondent at Piraeus.

We are going to have to ship the goods listed below, which are currently in transit at Piraeus, from there to Bern in Switzerland. Messrs. Paulino have told us that the shipping documents for this transaction are to be prepared at your end, and we would be grateful if you would kindly let us know what you can do to get them ready for shipment, and what you need from us.

Please note that our agents in Athens are J. Dianedes & Co., and that the bank handling the documents is the office of the National Bank of Greece in Plato St., Athens.

We look forward to hearing from you very soon on this subject, and thank you in advance for your co-operation.


*Explanations of reference numbers on pages 87–92*

[1] *per metric tonne or 10 cubic metres at steamer's option*: The shipowners can choose whether to charge freight on the weight or measurement; 10 cubic metres is taken as equivalent to 1 metric tonne.

[2] *commence loading*: Loading dates are given by shipowners so that the cargo can be assembled at the docks in good time.

[3] *closes for cargo*: A date is also given when the shipowners will accept no further cargo for that particular ship.

[4] *groupage rates*: Small consignments are sometimes 'grouped' together in one bill of lading; this is usually done by forwarding agents.

[5] *G.V.* (*grande vitesse*): The French term, in general use in Europe, for *fast goods*; P.V. (*petite vitesse*) indicates ordinary goods traffic. If no distinction is made in the rapidity of transport the term used is V.U. (*vitesse unique*).

[6] *routing order*: Instructions concerning the 'route' by which the consignment is to be sent: Dover/Dunkerque or Newhaven/Dieppe, etc.


# CHARTERING OF SHIPS

Chartering is a highly specialised business, but as far as correspondence is concerned we do not need to go into great detail, and the following is an outline of this side of the shipping business.

When the senders of goods have very large shipments to make, and especially when *bulk cargoes*[1] are concerned, it may be of greater advantage to them to have a whole ship at their disposal. They do not have to buy the ship but can hire it, and this is called 'chartering'. (The same word is also used for the hiring of a freight plane for the transport of merchandise.)

Some very large organisations have their own fleet of ships, especially when their raw material has to be shipped regularly from another part of the world; this is also the case when they specialise in one type of commodity, such as oil.

The chartering of ships is usually done through the intermediary of brokers, and in London there is a special centre called *the Baltic Exchange*[2] where the brokers operate, in much the same way as stock and share brokers on a stock exchange.

*Ship brokers* have an expert knowledge of rises and falls in rates for chartered ships, and the trends of the market. This is a very competitive business and there are no conferences to fix rates as in the case of the line companies: indeed, *tramp*[3] *rates* fluctuate very rapidly, according to supply and demand. The tramp market may be compared with the liner trade in much the same way as one can compare the cost of raw materials with a finished product; for example, the price of raw sugar varies almost daily whereas the price of a packet of manufactured sugar remains constant until the raw price becomes so high or so low that the retail price of sugar has to be altered.

The contract between the shipowner and the charterer is called the *charter party*, and it is, understandably, a long and rather complicated document. To facilitate cable communication, code names have been devised to indicate the type of trade concerned and the part of the world it relates to. For example: 'BALTCON' for Baltic & White Sea Conference Coal Charter. (These code names are listed in any book of shipping terms.)

A *charter party* may be for the carriage of goods from one specified port to another, and is known as a *voyage charter*, or it may cover a period of time and is known as a *time charter*. In the case of a voyage charter there is, on the back of the charter party, a form of the bill of lading, to cover the shipment of the cargo. In some cases the charterers may not need the complete space in the vessel and may agree to carry cargo also for other shippers.

It is obvious that certain cargoes, such as oil and coal, require special vessels for their transport (see glossary, page 96). Grain in bulk is carried in ships that can be loaded and unloaded by special apparatus—pouring the grain into the holds of the ship and sucking it out for unloading, which avoids the lengthy process of loading and unloading sacks (though this is still done sometimes).

Much of the business of chartering is done regularly by cable. The following are examples of the type of letters that would be required.

[10] *From charterers to brokers*

We are able to secure an order for 2,000 tons of coal and coke mixed, shipment Grimsby/Abo early next month. Please advise us of the lowest rate for a suitable fixture.[4]

## [11] *The broker's reply*

We thank you for your letter of 15 March, and confirm our cable of today reading as follows:

MV SCANDINAVIAN READY TO LOAD EARLY APRIL FULL CARGO AT £3.25 GRIMSBY ABO PLEASE CONFIRM CHARTERING IMMEDIATELY

As soon as we receive your instructions we shall be pleased to go ahead with the fixture.

## [12] *From charterers to brokers*

We have entered into a contract for the supply of motor vehicles and parts, over the next six months, to West Africa and shall be glad to know if you can fix us a time charter for a suitable vessel.

The question of speed must be considered as the ship should be able to make 3 voyages in the time, allowing . . . days for loading and unloading on each voyage.

In view of the general slackness of the market at the moment we hope that you can get us a really good offer.

## [13] *Reply from the brokers*

In confirmation of our cable to you today, a copy of which we enclose, we are pleased to say we have found what we think should be a very suitable vessel for your purpose: the *M.V. Mercury*, cargo capacity . . . tons, average speed . . . knots.

She is, perhaps, a little larger than you require, but the owners are prepared to consider a special rate for a time charter.

*Mercury* has just completed a charter and can therefore be at Liverpool dock and ready to load by the end of next week.

We hope this fixture will suit you, and as soon as we receive your confirmation we will prepare the charter party.

There is also a considerable business in the buying and selling of ships; the following letter is an example of such transactions.

## [14] *Offer of ship for sale (from ship brokers)*

We are pleased to inform you that we can now secure for sale the modern motor vessel *Hanoverian*, of which we enclose details.

The owners' ideas are about £. . ., on the basis of fairly prompt inspection and delivery U.K./Cont. port, but we would try for something less.

For your guidance, the vessel is now discharging at Plymouth docks, where she will be lying until 27 September. Prospective buyers may therefore inspect her in this port if they are prepared to decide immediately.

The owners are willing to give first-class buyers deferred terms of payment provided satisfactory guarantees are forthcoming.

We shall be pleased to hear if the vessel is of interest to you and we will then give you any further information you require.

## SHIP AGENTS

Ship agents—that is to say agents connected solely with ships, not forwarding agents—may offer their services for the loading and unloading of ships; the following is an example of this type of letter.

## [15] *Offer of services from ship agents*

We see from Lloyd's List that your *M.V. Orion* is expected to discharge at this port about the middle of next month, and we are writing to offer you our services as agents.

Our firm has had considerable experience, having been established here for 30 years, and we are acting as agents to all Anglo-Saxon chartered vessels calling at this port. We are also agents to a large number of European owners, as you will see from the enclosed list.

You can rely on us to secure your vessel a quick turn round,[5] and we might also mention that we can deal with all matters concerning crews, in accordance with . . . Articles.[6]

If you decide to let us have the agency we are sure that you will be fully satisfied with the results.

### *Explanations of reference numbers on pages 93–96*

[1] *bulk cargo*: This means that the goods do not require packing; such cargoes are usually coal, timber, oil, wheat, etc.

[2] *the Baltic Exchange* is so called because it started as a market for all kinds of produce from Baltic ports, which trade was extended to ships, insurance and aircraft.

[3] *tramp (trampship)*: This is a vessel that does not operate on a fixed route as a liner does. Probably derived from the name of a man who went about the country (tramped) working wherever there was work to be done.

[4] *fixture*: Particularly used in connection with chartering.

[5] *turn round*: As applied to a ship is the unloading, reloading and carrying out of the necessary formalities before the ship can sail again.

[6] *in accordance with . . . Articles*: This refers to the regulations laid down by different countries concerning the crews of their ships.

## GLOSSARY OF TRANSPORT TERMS

*Cost*

*carriage*: The word is used for inland transport and freight.

*cartage*: Short distance carriage.

*charges*: The price for services; also expenses, costs.

*drawback*: An allowance granted by the Customs on re-export of goods on which duty was paid on importation.

*dues*: Charges made by port authorities: dock dues, port dues.

*duty*: The tax levied on the import of goods.

*entry*: A word used by the Customs, referring to the particulars *entered* in a book; can be either *entry in* or *entry out*.

*freight*: The word is used for cost of transport *both inland and foreign*, also to mean the goods transported; freight train, air freight. *Deadfreight* is the cost of space booked but not used.

*lighterage*: Charge made for transporting goods by lighter, or barge.

*porterage*: Cost of hand transport, by porter.

*primage*: This is now used to mean a type of bonus to shippers.

*tariff*: The word used for a list of charges.

## Documents

*delivery order*: A document from the owner, or holder, of the goods requesting the release of goods held under warrant.

*dock warrant, warehouse warrant*: These are receipts issued for cargo deposited at dock warehouses.

*tally*: The record or list of cargo loaded or discharged; it is checked by a *tally clerk*, therefore *to tally* means to be correct.

## Names of various kinds of vessels

*coaster*: A ship on the coastal trade only.

*collier*: A ship that carries only coal and coke.

*craft*: Any kind of ship but usually means a small vessel.

*launch*: A small vessel for river and harbour transport; *to launch* is to float a newly-built ship for the first time.

*lighter*: Used in shipping for *barges*: cargo-carrying vessels on rivers and canals; *lighterman* is the name for the owner of lighters or the man in charge of a lighter.

*motor-ship*: A vessel driven by a motor.

*steamer, steamship*: A vessel driven by steam power.

*tanker*: A ship that carries bulk liquids, chiefly oil; the name is used also for road and rail vehicles that carry oil and bulk liquids.

*tug*: A small but powerful vessel that is used for *towing* other ships, either large or small (the word used as a verb means *to pull hard*).

## Dock terms

*berth*: A place at the quay, jetty or dockside where the ship may load, discharge or lie; the verb is *to berth*.

*bonded warehouse*: A store where goods are kept until the duty has been paid.

*bunkers*: The parts of the ship reserved for carrying the fuel needed; if the fuel is oil the name is *oil tanks*.

*crane, derrick*: Names used for lifting machinery in docks and on ships; also *hoist* and *tackle*.

*granaries*: Stores for grain, especially used in connection with the discharge from grain-carrying ships.

*lock*: A construction used for altering the level of the water in a dock, river or canal; it is also the space so controlled.

*quay*: The dockside where ships berth and goods are loaded or discharged.

*shed, store*: The building where the goods are kept (stored) before loading or after discharge; *transit shed* for goods to be transported to another place, *refrigerator store* for the storage of perishable goods.

*wharf, wharves*: Another name for a quay or quays, also including shed or sheds, etc. *Wharfage* is the charge for storing.

### Chartering terms

*demurrage*: The money paid to the shipowner if the charterer delays the sailing of the vessel.

*despatch money*: A bonus to the charterer for loading or unloading in less time than has been stipulated.

*lay days*: Days allowed for the loading and discharging of a ship.

*knot*: The speed of a ship, calculated as 1 nautical mile per hour.

*tonnage*: (1) Calculated as 100 cubic feet per ton to measure the ship's capacity, as (*a*) *gross tonnage*, and (*b*) *net registered tonnage* (N.R.T.) being the ship's cargo-carrying capacity; (2) Also used to mean all the ships belonging to a country.

### Names of firms and persons connected with transport

*common carriers*: Firms or organisations that undertake to carry goods for the general public.

*hauliers, haulage firms*: Contractors undertaking the transport of heavy goods by road.

*ship chandlers*: Suppliers of all the requirements of ships.

*stevedores*: (1) Contractors who arrange for the labour to load and discharge ships; (2) The men who actually do the work of loading and unloading, etc. (*Dockers* are all workers at docks.)

### Vehicles used on the roads and railways

*containers; lorries; tankers; trailers; trucks; vans; wagons.*

### Air

*airliner; passenger plane; freight plane.*

## LIABILITY OF TRANSPORT AND INSURANCE

Bills of lading, waybills and insurance policies contain many clauses concerning the contract of carriage and 'excepted perils'. There are four recognised headings under which most of them are grouped, stating the circumstances in which the carriers are not to be held liable:

*Act of God*: Natural perils that are beyond the control of man: earthquakes, storms, hurricanes, etc.

*Queen's enemies*: Losses that are due to enemy action; under this heading there are many subheadings.

*Inherent vice*: The capacity in the goods themselves of deterioration, as in: fruit, fish, meat, etc.

*Negligence*: The neglect of the shipper to pack suitably and sufficiently, or to notify shipowners and other carriers of the need for special care.

## EXERCISES

1. Fill in the missing words:

   Thank you _____ your enquiry _____ freight _____. We are enclosing details _____ our current _____ _____ standard containers _____ Liverpool _____ Amsterdam, and can _____ you that the *S.S. Lima* will be _____ cargo _____ Liverpool _____ 3 _____ 10 March _____.

   We also enclose our _____ card _____ the *Lima* and our _____ instructions _____. Will you please _____ the latter and _____ it to us as soon as possible.

2. Write to a firm of shipping agents in England and ask them to quote you for the collection of some cases of tools from a firm in Birmingham, and the shipment to your nearest port.

3. As a firm of forwarding agents you have been asked to advise on the forwarding of a consignment of bicycles. Write a suitable letter and ask by what route the bicycles are to be sent; give your advice on the matter.

4. You have been asked to arrange for a consignment of goods by train-ferry; reply to the letter and point out that the consignment must be over 1 ton in weight. Advise alternative routes.

5. Write to the office of British Airways and ask for particulars of freight, insurance, etc., on a consignment of watches and clocks.

6. Write a letter to your customers informing them what arrangements you have made for the transport of a consignment of chemicals. Your customers may be in America or another country outside Europe.

7. Confirm a telegram you have sent to customers, in which you stated there was a delay in the sailing of the ship; say what you are doing to hasten the despatch of the consignment.

8. Write to a firm of shipping agents and ask them to take charge of a consignment you have shipped to an overseas country; say who will take delivery of the goods.

9. Write to ship brokers and ask them to charter a ship for the loading of a cargo of fertilisers; give them necessary particulars about port and time.

10. Write a letter from ship brokers, concerning the shipment of goods to Canada and pointing out the need for speed because of the probable closing of certain ports through ice.

11. As ship brokers, write to customers who may be interested in the purchase of a vessel; give such particulars as may be necessary.

# 9 | Banking and payments in foreign trade

The purpose of this chapter is not to deal with all the numerous functions of banking, but to outline the principal services rendered by banks in connection with trade, and to give the reader the vocabulary and phraseology which is essential for correspondence and for an understanding of the various documents used in matters relating to payments in commerce.

The main functions of banks are to accept and hold deposits, to honour drafts—cheques and bills of exchange—drawn on them, and to grant advances in the form of loans and overdrafts. Banks also provide services such as keeping customers' accounts, obtaining and giving information, transferring funds for payments or investments, handling foreign currency transactions, issuing letters of credit, acting as trustees, executors and guarantors, looking after securities and other valuables, and, in foreign trade, collecting payments, discounting bills of exchange, and financing imports and exports.

Dealings with banks tend to be rather formal, since such business is confidential and is conducted according to a very strict code of conduct, and it is inevitable that this formality should be reflected in correspondence between banks and their customers. So we may reasonably expect some of the old *commercialese* of the nineteenth and early twentieth centuries to survive in letters written to and by banks, and, in fact, we do. The survival of this formal phraseology has a great advantage in modern commerce: its meaning is perfectly clear to everyone involved in transactions with banks, both at home and abroad.

Nevertheless, banks are commercial institutions, and as such they have to sell their services. No bank today can afford to rely exclusively on large customers, and in Britain there has in recent years been a great deal of competition for the custom of small savers. Correspondence has accordingly been modified so as to appeal to the man in the street, and the language of letters written by banks is now closer to the spoken language than it has ever been.

## A SHORT EXPLANATION OF SOME BANKING TERMS

*Current account*: The account into which a client pays his trading receipts and on which he draws his cheques. No interest is paid on a current account. Banks make charges for handling these accounts unless an agreed minimum balance is kept in over an agreed period of time.

*Deposit account*: Surplus funds from the current account are held in this, and receive interest.

*Interest*: The charge or profit due for lending money.

*Loan*: Money lent ((*v.*) lend, borrow; (*n.*) lender, borrower). Banks *lend to* their customers. Customers *borrow from* their banks.

*Cheque*: An order in writing from a person to his bank to pay on demand a certain sum to a named person.

*Bill of exchange*: An order in writing from one person to a bank or to another person, to pay on demand or at a given date, a certain sum to the person named in the bill.

*Letter of credit* (*commercial*): An arrangement with a bank by means of which a buyer guarantees payment to a seller on fulfilment by the seller of certain agreed conditions. The instruction must be in writing and if marked 'irrevocable', it cannot be cancelled.

*Draft*: This really means a document used to 'draw' money from some source, but sometimes it is used to refer to the money itself. A bill of exchange is often referred to in a letter as 'the draft'.

*Banker's draft*: A draft or cheque drawn by one bank on another.

*Banker's transfer*: Transfer of money from the bank account of a debtor to the bank account of his creditor by order of the debtor.

*Overdraft*: A debit balance on a bank customer's current account. This may be authorised by the bank.

*Security*: A document of value given as cover for a loan. (Collateral security = additional or supporting cover).

*Trustee*: Person appointed to protect the interests and property of a person unable to do so for himself.

*Executor*: Person appointed to carry out the wishes of another person deceased.

## CORRESPONDENCE WITH BANKS

The private nature of much of the business done with banks reduces correspondence with them chiefly to routine matters, formal instructions, advice and requests for information. Much of this, too, is done by special forms. Confidential matters are usually dealt with in interviews between bank managers and their clients, a practice actively encouraged by British banks.

The following phrases and sentences are those commonly used in connection with routine correspondence.

## Opening an account

1. Please open a current account for us in the name of John Smith & Co. We enclose specimen signatures of the partners, either of whom may sign cheques on our behalf. Will you kindly open our no. 1 account with £750 and place £250 to our credit in a no. 2 account.
2. To open the account we enclose a cheque on the XYZ Bank for £. . .
3. Kindly open the account in my name. I am instructing my bank . . ., to transfer the equivalent of S. Fr. . . . for this purpose.
4. Please advise us of the present interest rate on deposit accounts and approximately what balance you require us to keep in our current account to eliminate charges.

## Payment instructions

5. Please transfer £100 to the Westland Bank Ltd., Bournsea, to the credit of Clark & Sons Ltd., debiting our no. 1 account.
6. Kindly effect the following payments for us: . . .
7. Please transfer the sterling equivalent of DM 1250 to Postscheckkonto Hamburg XXX in favour of Gebrueder Mueller, Hamburg, Hohestr. 1122. This sum represents payment for costs incurred by that firm on our behalf.
8. Please pay to the XYZ Banking Corporation on the 15th of each month and till further notice, the sum of £. . . for the account of John Brown.
9. With effect from 1 January will you please discontinue payments to the Great Eastern Bank authorised in our letter of 1 June last.
10. Referring to the instructions regarding payment to J. J. Hooper Ltd., and contained in our letter of 3 April 1977, we now wish you to cancel these.
11. Kindly cancel the credit opened in favour of Miss . . . as alternative arrangements have been made.
12. Please withhold payment of £500 deposit to Messrs. . . . as the purchase of the equipment concerned may not now be made. We will keep you informed of any developments.
13. We have to ask you to stop payment of our cheque no. . . . drawn on 23 September in favour of Johnson Bros., until further notice.
14. Please suspend payment of our cheque no. . . . drawn in favour of Messrs. Pink & Brown, as it appears to have been lost in the post.

## Accounting and special instructions

15. Thank you for your advice of receipt of £235 from The XXX Banking Corporation on behalf of Mr Jacques. This item should have been credited to our no. 2 account and we shall be glad if you will make the necessary transfer.
16. With reference to sheet no. 15 of your statement of our current account, we have no record of the cheque no. 1111 for which you show a debit of £101.53. Will you kindly examine this entry or send a copy of the cheque for our inspection.
17. Kindly give us details of your credit entries for £23.53 and £123.88 on 2 June and 5 June respectively, items for which we have received no credit advice from you.
18. Will you please inform us what services are covered by your entry 'Special Charges' dated 1 January.
19. We are pleased to say that our records now agree with your statement.
20. Kindly credit all sums received under £25 to our no. 2 account. Please also transfer £500 from our current account to deposit account.
21. Please purchase at the best possible rate the following foreign currency, and debit to our current account:

## [1] *Bank customer requests an overdraft*

The Manager,
Southland Bank Ltd.
Westerham,
Kent K32 GN4

Dear Sir

Further to our interview of yesterday, I request your permission to overdraw my account up to a limit of £1,000 between 1 January and 1 August 19. . . .

As I explained to you yesterday, I have during this period to meet certain capital costs incurred in the expansion of my business. The benefit of this expansion will not be felt till around 30 June, when considerable sums will be due to me from home and overseas customers. As security, share certificates worth £500 will be deposited with you and a life endowment policy for £300 will be assigned to you.

I look forward to an early reply.

Yours faithfully

J. THOMAS

## [2] *Bank's reply to request for an overdraft*

Dear Mr Thomas

I have given your letter careful consideration and agree to grant you an overdraft of £1,000 available till 1 August 19. . ., subject to the usual proviso[1] that there is no change in the position as at present existing.

Will you please therefore let me have the securities mentioned in your letter; it will be in order for you meanwhile to anticipate[2] the overdraft.

Interest will be charged at 11 % and will be calculated on the daily balances. I rely on you to clear the outstanding balance by 1 August, and I trust you will be successful in expanding your trade.

Yours sincerely

D. L. ROSE

*Manager*

## PAYMENTS IN FOREIGN TRADE

Paying for goods supplied in the home trade is a fairly simple matter. Payment is made either in advance or within a reasonably short period after delivery. There is little time lost in correspondence and in delivery, as a result of which most suppliers can afford to give the required short credit of one month usual in home trading.

Payment follows by cheque or draft, and the whole transaction is speedily concluded. If a buyer fails to pay, legal action is reasonably quick and payment can be enforced. Even so, the granting of credit entails its own problems, and as modern trade depends on credit, this always needs careful handling.

These problems are magnified many times in foreign trade. A great deal of time is unavoidably spent on correspondence, despatch and delivery. Who is to bear this loss? Must the seller wait perhaps 6 months for his money—or is the buyer to pay several months before he even sees his goods? Further, in a case of non-payment, a seller will be involved in expensive legal action and possibly total loss.

It is here that banks play a vital part. Their services to exporters and importers include:

1. Handling of shipping documents.
2. Collection of payments.
3. Observance of buyers' conditions of purchase.
4. Discounting bills of exchange.
5. Loans to exporters.
6. Acting as agents for foreign banks and their customers.

By means of these services banks not only see to it that justice is done to both buyer and seller, but that the timelag[3] between order and delivery is overcome without loss to either party. These services have to be paid for, but are not expensive and are almost indispensable—the bank comes into every transaction at some stage or another.

Payments in foreign trade may be made by:

1. Banker's transfer.
2. Bill of exchange.
3. Letter of credit.

Also, as in the home trade, payment may be made

(a) in advance;

(b) on open account.

Payment in advance might be helpful to a buyer in urgent need, or where the buyer is unknown to the seller, or in the case of a single isolated transaction. The actual method of payment in such cases would probably be by banker's draft or banker's transfer.

Open account terms would be granted by a seller to a buyer of unquestioned standing or to a customer in whom he has complete confidence, e.g. regular buyers, agents or distributors. Payment might then be made quarterly by bill of exchange or banker's transfer.

## THE BANKER'S TRANSFER

This is a simple transference of money from the bank account of a buyer in his own country to the bank account of the seller in the seller's country. It is merely necessary for the buyer or a debtor to send a letter of instruction to his bank—or use a special form. The transfer is carried out at current rates of exchange. Such transfers are, of course, subject to any exchange control regulations of the countries concerned. This transaction is simple and quick and can be speeded up by cabled instructions if desired.

104

# THE BILL OF EXCHANGE (B/E)

The full story of the bill of exchange is too long for inclusion in this book and the reader should study it in one of the many works in English on commercial practice.

In brief, the bill is an order in writing from a creditor to a debtor to pay on demand or on a named date a certain sum of money to a person named on the bill, or to his order. The bill is drawn by the creditor on the debtor, and is sent to the debtor (or his agent) for the latter to pay or *accept* (i.e. to acknowledge the debt). The debtor accepts by signing his name on the face (i.e. front) of the bill, together with the date. The bill now becomes legally binding, and the acceptor must meet it on or before the due date.

The creditor (the *drawer*) can order the debtor (the *drawee*) to pay the money to any bank named by him on the bill. The drawee, in accepting the bill, can add the name of the bank which he wishes to pay the bill. In this case, the bill stays with the drawer's bank till due for payment, when it will be presented to the paying bank for settlement. Such a bill is said to be *domiciled* with the holding bank.

---

| No 101 | £ 169·00 | London, 20th August, 1977 |

_____ 60 days _____ after sight of this first of
Exchange (second and third of the same tenor and
date unpaid) pay to the order of _____

_____ Modern Implements Ltd _____

_____ One hundred and sixty nine pounds _____
value received, payable at the current rate of
Exchange for Bankers' sight drafts on London.

To L. Petersen Ltd
   Copenhagen

For and on behalf of
MODERN IMPLEMENTS LTD.

JJSmith

Director

---

An important feature of the bill of exchange is that it is *negotiable*, which means that it can be used by the holder to pay debts of his own, or in other words, he can *negotiate* it. To do this, the holder must *endorse* it, i.e. sign his name on the back of the bill before passing it on to the new holder.

Other ways in which the holder can use a bill are:
1. Sell it to a bank, who will pay face value, less interest: this is called *discounting* a bill.
2. Leave it with a bank as security for a loan.

It is this free negotiability of the bill which makes it a practical means of payment in foreign trade. Of course, its successful operation depends on confidence and trust. Each individual firm's standing and reputation is known and taken into account in handling bills.

The advantages of the bill will be clear to a student who understands something of modern commerce; perhaps the two chief assets are: (*a*) it simplifies the financing of export and import trade; (*b*) it saves innumerable individual money transactions, or movements of currency.

Failure to meet a bill on the due date would result in total discredit for the drawee, and legal action can follow. An unpaid bill is said to be *dishonoured*, and the drawer can *protest* it, which clears the way for him to *prosecute* (i.e. take legal action against) the drawee.

(*See end of this chapter for special terminology*)

## THE LETTER OF CREDIT (L/C)

The most generally used method of payment in the export trade today is the letter of credit. It is ideal for individual transactions or for a series, makes trade with unknown buyers easy, gives protection to both seller and buyer and overcomes the *credit gap* (i.e. the time-payment loss between order and delivery).

A letter of credit starts with the buyer. He instructs his bank to *issue* the L/C for the amount of the purchase and in favour of the seller. This is usually done by special printed form. (*See specimen on page 107*) The instruction, or form, contains full details of the transaction as agreed between buyer and seller. The buyer's bank sends these instructions to its agent (i.e. a bank co-operating with it) in the seller's country. On receiving these instructions, the agent bank writes to advise the seller of the credit. In foreign trade it is normal for the agent bank to *confirm* the credit. This means that the agent bank undertakes to pay the seller the money due to him, provided the conditions set out in the L/C have been complied with. The seller can now execute the buyer's order, knowing that when he has done so, the money will be paid at once by the agent bank. The buyer is equally secure, because the agent bank will pay on his behalf only if the conditions of the transaction are fully carried out by the seller. For this reason, great care and accuracy are needed in giving the original instructions.

It is not essential that a L/C be paid to the seller immediately upon execution of the order. If agreed between seller and buyer, the arrangement could be for the agent bank to accept a B/E drawn by the seller on the agent bank. This gives the buyer credit and is, of course, absolutely safe for the seller, who can discount the bill for ready cash if he needs it.

From these outlines of the methods used in financing foreign trade, the student will realise the vital part played by banks; without them, modern trade could not exist. Their services are paid for by their *charges* and these are kept low by the *security* they normally require against the risks taken.

*Note*: American importers often open the letter of credit at an American bank. This bank then confirms the credit to the foreign seller and requests him to draw on them for the amount of the invoice, and to send them all documents required by the buyer.

Form 99 (1975)

Duplicate to Overseas Dept., Import Credits Section, London/Chief Accountant's Dept., Head Office (*Delete as appropriate*)

Application for Documentary Credit – Request and Indemnity ①

To: **LLOYDS BANK LIMITED**      Advise by: *Airmail/Telex or Urgent/Ordinary/Cheap Rate Cable quoting full/brief details

*Delete inappropriate words.

Please open on our account a Credit in the following terms:

(i)  State whether
     (a) Revocable
     (b) Irrevocable or
     (c) Irrevocable and Confirmed by Correspondent

1.  This Credit is to be (i) ②

2.  and advised through (*Correspondent*) (ii) _____

N.B.  If Credit is to be transferable see Note 12 on reverse.

3.  In favour of (*Beneficiary*) ③
    (*Address*)

(ii)  Fill in ONLY when Correspondents especially nominated. See Note 2 on reverse.

4.  To the extent of _____ ④ (*in words*)

5.  The Credit is to expire on _____ in _____ (State Town/Country)
    (*Unless previously cancelled – if Credit is revocable*)

6.  The Credit is to be available by the beneficiary's draft(s)
    *(a)  at _____ sight in sterling/currency on Lloyds Bank Limited, London.
    *(b)  at _____ sight in currency on the Correspondent.
    As regards (b) where payment is to be made at sight, the beneficiary's draft need not be presented.

(iii)  For less than full invoice value delete and give instructions under 12.

Drafts to be drawn/payments to be made for the full invoice value and submitted with the under-mentioned documents attached (iii).

7.  Documents required:-
    (a)  Invoice
    (b)  Policy or Certificate of Insurance in the same currency as the Credit for C.I.F. Invoice value plus _____ per cent covering Marine and War Risks and also _____ (iv).
         (If shipment effected in a Container this must be indicated on the insurance document).

(iv)  If insurance documents are not required state who is covering insurance or If insurance is to be effected in a currency different from that of the Credit the wording of 7(b) must be altered accordingly.

    (c)  *Complete set of clean "On Board" Shipping Company's Bills of Lading/Shipping Company's Combined Transport Bills of Lading made out to order and endorsed in blank marked Freight Paid/Freight Payable at Destination.
         Documents must be presented to the paying/accepting/negotiating bank not later than _____ days after the date of the Bills of Lading or other shipping documents stated herein and within the credit validity.
    (d)

8.  Covering Shipment of:-

9.  Price      *FOB/C & F/CIF

10.  Shipment from      to

11.  *Partial shipment allowed/prohibited
     *Transhipment allowed/prohibited

12.  Special Instructions (*if any*)

(v)  Please complete "Exchange Control" details overleaf.

13.  We give overleaf the information required for Exchange Control purposes and we agree to pay you a commission of _____ % (minimum £ _____ for each three months or part thereof for this Credit and when applicable an acceptance commission of _____ % per month minimum two months minimum £ _____ (v).

1.  The documents and the goods and all proceeds of sales thereof and of insurances thereon and all our rights as unpaid sellers shall be security to you for all obligations and liabilities incurred by you or Correspondents in connection with this Credit and for all disbursements in connection with the goods or otherwise (which we hereby authorise you to pay for our account) and all other our liabilities to you present and future.

2.  You may on payment debit our account with all sums paid in connection with this Credit or the goods, also with any commission and interest, or with the whole or part of the amount of the Credit at any time if you think fit, and on demand we will place you in funds to meet such debits, and we will at the latest place you in funds to meet any acceptances three days before their due date or earlier if required. In the case of Credits in foreign currency you may pass any such debits in sterling at your rate of exchange, and if passed after payment, at your rate ruling when you receive advice of payment unless otherwise arranged. In the event of any default you may sell the documents or goods before or after arrival, and any deficit we will pay you on demand, and we will indemnify you against all claims, demands, costs, charges and expenses incurred in connection with this Credit.

3.  Your rights against us hereunder shall not be affected by, and you and/or Correspondents shall not be responsible for, any loss or damage to the goods however and whenever caused, their quantity, quality, condition or their detention by any person whatsoever or howsoever caused, the loss, validity, sufficiency, genuineness or accuracy of the shipping, insurance or any other documents or failure from any reason by you, Correspondents or any other person to store protect or insure the goods, and all acts and omissions of the drawers and/or Vendors and/or Correspondents and/or any other persons shall be at our risk.

4.  If the Credit is revocable it may be cancelled by you at any time, but cancellation by you or by us shall be without prejudice to our respective obligations as regards any bills negotiated or accepted or payments made thereunder before notice of such cancellation has been received at the place where the Credit is available.

5.  All cables/telex messages in connection with this Credit shall be despatched at our risk and cost and you shall not be responsible for any loss caused by mistakes, mutilations or omissions in their transmission coding or decoding or interpretation when received or by delay on the part of the cable or telegraph companies concerned.

6.  If two or more parties sign this document the obligations hereunder are joint and several.

7.  This Credit is to be subject to the Uniform Customs and Practice for Documentary Credits (1974 revision) International Chamber of Commerce Publication No. 290.

Accounter's Name and Signature.

Date _____

NOTE FOR BRANCH MANAGERS. – A copy of this form as signed to be sent to the Overseas Department or Chief Accountant's Department (if beneficiary in U.K. or Eire). If the instructions are telegraphed/telephoned to one of those Departments the copy should follow by post marked clearly "Confirmation of Telegram/Telephone". INSURANCE. – If Insurance documents are not called for, the Branch Manager should confirm below under "Remarks" that he is satisfied that the Insurance is actually covered and available for the Bank's protection.
The above instructions are confirmed.  (STATE HOW SANCTIONED)

M.D.P. £ _____

BRANCH
BRANCH CODE NUMBER

MANAGER

107

Explanation of reference numbers on the form:

1. *Indemnity*: Release from liability. (*Note*: Indemnity clauses are not reproduced in the above form.)
2. *Correspondents*: The buyer's agent (if any) in seller's country.
3. *Beneficiary*: The seller.
4. The amount to be paid is given here.

## CORRESPONDENCE BETWEEN BUYERS AND SELLERS

### Bills: (1) The buyer writes to the seller

22. Please draw on us for the amount of your invoice and attach the documents listed below to your draft.
23. We propose to pay by bill of exchange at 30 d/s, documents against acceptance. Please confirm if this is acceptable to you.
24. You may draw on our London agents, Messrs. . . . at 60 d/s for the amount of your invoice. Our agents have been instructed accordingly and advised of the terms of our agreement.
25. We have received your letter and invoice dated 3 January and are willing to accept your draft for the amount involved, payable at 60 days' sight.
26. Our bankers in Hamburg, Die Handelsbank, will accept your draft on them on our behalf.
27. We agree to accept the goods in 3 shipments and you may draw on us at 90 days from date of despatch in the case of each shipment.
28. Kindly send us 2 bills of lading by separate posts, together with your draft at 60 days for acceptance.
29. Our acceptances will be honoured at . . . Bank on presentation.
30. Your draft of 25 April has been accepted and will be given our protection.[4]
31. Your draft on us for £250 in favour of J. J. Brown has been accepted, but will you please note that such drafts should be advised in future.
32. In view of the current low level of prices we have to ask you to limit your drafts on us to 60% of the amount you expect us to obtain for your consignments, or we shall be unable to meet these drafts.
33. I am very sorry to say that I find myself unable to meet this bill, due on 1 December, and I feel sure you will appreciate the difficulty in which I am placed. If you would kindly accept £300 cash and draw a further bill on me at 2 months for the balance of £150 plus interest at 6%, I would be most grateful to you and guarantee to honour it on presentation.
34. We are surprised to find that you have drawn on us for the last shipment, as we advised you in our letter of 11 February that we could handle these goods on a <u>consignment basis</u>[5] only. Please note that we have accordingly declined to accept your bill in this instance. *without fixed price*
35. Your draft for the shipment by *S.S. Calcutta* was presented yesterday and duly met. We should now like to ask you if you are willing to supply us in future on 60 d/s, D/A terms, as other suppliers in your country are already allowing us this credit. *documents against acceptance*
36. The goods arrived in excellent condition and we are fully satisfied with them. If you can guarantee to repeat this quality we shall place large orders with you, and in this case we shall require open account terms. Please let us know if you are prepared to grant us these, with settlement by banker's transfer within 30 days of date of your quarterly statement.

*the drawee must pay the bill of each before the bank will give him the doc that he needs to get the possession of the goods.*

37. In reply to your letter of . . . in which you say that our acceptance no. 1210 of 22 June appears to have been lost in a plane crash, we are willing to accept a copy of this provided you indemnify us against liability in the event of the original being found.

## Bills: (2) The seller writes to the buyer

38. In accordance with our (terms of payment) (agreement) we have drawn on you at 30 days' sight for the amount of the enclosed invoice.
39. Your proposal to pay by draft is acceptable to us and we shall accordingly draw on you at 2 months from date of shipment of your order.
40. As arranged, we are attaching our sight draft on you for £310 to the shipping documents and are handing them to our bank for forwarding to you.
41. We note that you wish us to draw on your London agents for the amount of our invoice. This is acceptable to us and we shall send them our draft for attention as soon as the goods are ready for shipment.
42. We have pleasure in advising you that your order no. . . . was despatched on the *S. S. Banji* on 20 April and you should receive the goods within 3 weeks. Our draft on you at 60 d/s in favour of R. A. Mason will be presented to you by the Great Oriental Bank, Shanghai, and we would be grateful if you would kindly give it your protection.
43. We are pleased to confirm that each shipment will be separately charged and that we shall draw on you under advice[6] for the invoice amounts.
44. We apologise for our failure to advise you that we had drawn on you. This was due to a misunderstanding and we shall take care to avoid any recurrence.
45. In view of the recent price fluctuations in your market we shall not draw on you till we have your first reports on the prices you are obtaining for these goods.
46. We are quite willing to put your account on a 60 d/s D/A basis and will make this effective from 1 January.
47. Your request for open account terms has been considered and we are pleased to grant this facility. We would, however, prefer to draw a sight bill on you quarterly in favour of the Export Bank of Australia, and we hope this will be agreeable to you.
48. Much to our surprise, our draft on you dated 11 May and due 1 July was returned dishonoured yesterday by our bank. Having received no communication from you at any time since the despatch of the goods covered by this draft, we must ask you for an immediate explanation. Meanwhile we are requesting our bank to re-present the draft.

## Bills: (3) Letters to and from the bank
## (Seller—to his bank)

49. We enclose our sight draft on Ajax & Co. Ltd. of Cape Town and attach bill of lading to evidence shipment, and other documents as listed below. Will you please deliver these documents to Ajax against payment of the draft, and credit our account no. 1 with the amount received.
50. Will you please forward the enclosed sight draft on Messrs. . . . to The Regal Banking Co. of Toronto, Canada, with instructions to surrender the attached documents on payment of our bill.
51. Kindly instruct your correspondent in Zurich to release the documents to the drawee only on settlement of our sight draft for £. . . .
52. Please credit our no. 2 account with the proceeds[7] after deducting your charges.
53. Please note that all charges are for the account of the drawee.
54. Kindly advise us of the amount of your charges, for inclusion in our draft.
55. Please surrender the enclosed documents to our customer on acceptance of the attached draft on him at 60 days for £750.
56. The invoice and documents covering a shipment of steel tubing for The Union Con-

struction Co., Bombay, are enclosed. Our draft for £972 on this firm, due at 3 months, is also enclosed, and we ask you to present this for acceptance against surrender of documents and to collect the amount due <u>at maturity</u>. *p de verwaldag*

57. Please present the bill for acceptance and then discount it at the current rate, for the credit of our account.

58. Our export trade in nylon tubes and piping is increasing rapidly and we are no longer able to finance this trade ourselves. Are you willing to advance us up to 70% of the value of our overseas orders on production of the invoice and bill of lading? Our drafts on our customers would be passed to you with the documents, of course. We should appreciate details of your services and charges in connection with business of this type.

59. We enclose various acceptances as listed below. Kindly present them for payment at due date and credit the proceeds to our account.

60. We enclose a sight draft for $10,000 to your order on The Aluminium Fittings Corporation of Pittsburgh. Please make the following payments to our various American creditors against this draft: . . .

61. Please give us details of your collection charges for drafts on European and South American import merchants.

*(Seller—to foreign bank)*

62. Messrs. J. & A. Lotham of 53 High Street, Liverpool, have asked us to draw on you at 2 months for S. Fr. 50,200 in respect of a shipment of textiles as per invoice attached. Our draft for this amount is enclosed together with the shipping documents. Will you please accept the draft and return it to us, at the same time sending the documents to Messrs. Lotham.

63. Our agents in New York will shortly be sending you the shipping documents covering a consignment of books. Will you please release these documents to Messrs. . . . against their payment of the attached sight draft on them for $3,000. Please hold the funds pending disposal instructions. *instructies in de in afwachting van de verhandeling*

*(Buyer—to his bank)*

64. The following drafts will shortly be presented to you by foreign drawers. Please accept them on my behalf and meet them at maturity to the debit of my no. 2 account. Your charges are for the account of the drawers.

65. I enclose an accepted bill drawn on me by Fa. Antonio and should be glad to receive the documents covering the goods in question. *domicilieren (te /adlbaar stellen)*

66. Please note that we have <u>domiciled</u> the following acceptances with you: Will you kindly honour them at due date and advise us at time of payment.

67. Can you please make arrangements with a bank in West Berlin for the payment of our Eastern European suppliers' drafts on us? Your <u>advice</u> on the necessary formalities would be appreciated. *bericht*

# THE LETTER OF CREDIT

Perhaps the most interesting way to study the correspondence of the L/C would be to follow a transaction from order to payment. Let us suppose that the Jameson Construction Company of Durban, South Africa, needs aluminium fittings and has already made an enquiry to the Aluminium Alloy Co. Ltd. of Birmingham, England. They now decide to place the order and do so in accordance with the price quotations already made by

the sellers. At the same time they decide to pay by letter of credit, payable in London and available by draft on a London bank at 60 days' sight.
They write this letter to their suppliers:

## THE JAMESON CONSTRUCTION
### CO. LTD.
Durban, S.A.

The Aluminium Alloy Co. Ltd.                                      3 August 1978
Birmingham

Dear Sirs

Many thanks for your letter of 30 June enclosing your catalogue
and details of your terms. We have decided to place the attached
order with you and would be glad if you would give it your early
attention.

We have instructed The General Bank of South Africa to open a credit
for £625 in your favour, valid until 15 September. The credit will be
confirmed by The General Bank of South Africa, Clements Lane, London,
who will accept your draft on them at 60 days for the amount of your
invoice. Please attach the following documents to your draft:

> 2 bills of lading,
> 2 commercial invoices,
> Insurance policy for £700.

Despatch and marking instructions will be given by our forwarding agents
in London, who will advise you of their charges. Your invoice should
include c.i.f. Durban, and the amount of our credit is sufficient to
cover this and your bank commission on the draft.

Please advise us by airmail when the goods have been despatched.

Yours faithfully

*John Smith*

THE JAMESON CONSTRUCTION COMPANY LTD.

## 3

The Jameson Construction Co. open the L/C by writing to their bankers, The General Bank of South Africa, Durban, giving full instructions, or by using a form something like that printed on page 107. That bank then notifies the credit to their branch in London. Meanwhile, The Aluminium Alloy Co. Ltd. receives the order and acknowledges it:

Aluminium Alloy Co. Ltd.  Birmingham

79 Prince Albert St.     Birmingham B21 8DJ     Great Britain

The Jameson Construction Co. Ltd.        10 August 1978
Durban S.A.


Dear Sirs

We are very pleased to have your order and are able to confirm that all the items required are in stock.  It is a pleasure to have the opportunity of supplying you and we are quite sure you will be satisfied both with the quality of our goods and our service.

Your choice of method of payment is quite acceptable to us, and we note that this will be by irrevocable letter of credit for a sum not exceeding £625, valid till September 15th.  When we receive confirmation of this credit from The General Bank of South Africa, London, we will make up your order and await despatch instructions from your agent.

We assure you that this order and all further orders made will have our immediate attention.

Yours faithfully

THE ALUMINIUM ALLOY CO. LTD.

## 4

A copy of the form used by The Jameson Construction Co. is meanwhile sent by the branch of The General Bank of South Africa in Durban to the London branch of this bank to authorise the opening of the credit.

The next step is, of course, for the London branch of The General Bank of South Africa to advise The Aluminium Alloy Co. that the credit is available (i.e. to confirm the credit). Here again, a form may be used. If, however, advice is by letter it would read something like this:

## THE GENERAL BANK OF SOUTH AFRICA
## LONDON

16 August 1978

The Aluminium Alloy Co. Ltd.
Birmingham.

Dear Sirs

We have received instructions from The General Bank of South Africa, Durban, to open an irrevocable letter of credit for £625 in your favour and valid till 15 September, 1978. You are authorised to draw a 60 days' bill on us against this credit for the amount of your invoice after shipment of various metal fittings as list enclosed and consigned to The Jameson Construction Co. of Durban, South Africa, has been effected. We shall require the documents listed below to be produced by you before we accept your draft, which should include all charges to Durban and our discount commission at 6%. It is also stipulated by the buyer that the goods covered by this draft be despatched in one shipment.

Yours faithfully

M. J. LOWE

Manager

(List of documents)

When the order has been collected, marked and shipped by the forwarding agent, who sends his note of charges with the insurance policy and the various other documents to The Aluminium Alloy Co. Ltd., the latter sends the documents to The General Bank of South Africa (London).

[6]

## THE ALUMINIUM ALLOY CO. LTD.
## BIRMINGHAM

5 September 1978

The Manager
The General Bank of South Africa
Clements Lane
London EC3 4WE

Ref.: LC/1001/16./8.

Dear Sir

Referring to your advice of 16 August we now have pleasure in enclosing the shipping documents as called for in your letter.

As required by your customer, we have included all charges in our invoice, which amounts to £601.53. Our draft on you for this amount is enclosed, and we ask you to discount it, after acceptance, at the agreed rate. Kindly remit the net amount to our no. 2 account at The South Midland Bank, Birmingham.

We thank you for your assistance in the matter.

Yours faithfully

THE ALUMINIUM ALLOY CO. LTD.

113

Form No. 123A
1978 SB

‡Without recourse confirmed and irrevocable

‡If the condition "without recourse" is not applicable delete the reference thereto and initial.
This form is to be used only between Branches and the Bank's offices in the United Kingdom, the Continent of Europe, and the United States of America.

3 August, 1978

To the Manager of

# The General Bank Limited,

D U R B A N ............................ Branch.

## Confirmed Irrevocable Letter of Credit for £ 625    No. 1

1. X/We hereby authorise THE ALUMINIUM ALLOY CO. LTD.
of BIRMINGHAM, ENGLAND .......... to draw at 60 days ............................ sight on me/us to the extent of SIX HUNDRED AND TWENTY FIVE POUNDS
............................ (£ 625 ............)
in one or more draft, in favour of **The General Bank Limited,** for invoice cost of
............ ALUMINIUM FITTINGS ............
(Insert brief description of merchandise.)
to be shipped C & F./C.I.F./F.O.B. per Steamer and/or Motor Vessel from LONDON
to DURBAN ............ such draft(s) and relative shipping documents to be
presented at † THE GENERAL BANK LIMITED, LONDON.
for negotiation on or before 15 September, 1978
†State here the name of the office or agency of the Bank at which the drafts are to be negotiated, or if the applicant desires the credit to be made available at a Branch of a foreign Bank, indicate the Bank and the particular office concerned.

2. And I/we hereby agree with the Drawers, Endorsers and *bona fide* holders of such Draft(s) to pay at sight or to accept it/them on presentation if drawn at a currency and pay it/them at maturity, together with Exchange, Dominion, Colonial or other stamps and other usual and proper charges on or in connection with such Draft(s).

3. Draft(s) under this Credit is/xxx to be accompanied by a complete set of shipping documents, consisting of:—
   (a) Full set of negotiable clean "On Board" Bills of Lading marked freight paid to order of shippers and endorsed in blank. xxxxxxxxxxxxxxxxxxxxx
   (N.B.—Bills of Lading which do not clearly indicate that goods are actually on board steamer and/or motor vessel, before expiry date of this Credit, are inadmissible.)
   (b) Certified Customs Invoice(s) in duplicate for face value of the Draft(s). Freight (if applicable), cartage, commission, Bank exchange, cost of insurance and incidentals may be included in the invoice cost of the goods.
   (c) Marine and War Risks Insurance Policies or Certificates in duplicate endorsed in blank, for not less than the full C.I.F. invoice value of the shipment in British Sterling, or in U.S.A. or Canadian Dollars if the amount of the Letter of Credit is expressed payable in either of those currencies.
   (N.B.—Insurances may be effected with Foreign Companies but must be in British Sterling or United States of America or Canadian Dollars. The Bank is hereby authorised to reserve to itself the right to reject insurance documents if not satisfied with the standing of the Insurers.)

4. xxxxxxxxxxxxxxxxxxxxxxxxxxxxxxxxxxxxxxxxxxxxxxxxxxxxxxxxxxxxxxxxxxxxxxxxxxxxxxx xxxxxxxxxxxxxxxxxxxxxxxxxxxxxxxxxxxxxxxxxxxxxxxxxxxxxxxxxxxxxxxxxxxxx xxxxxxxxxxx

5. Transhipment at CAPE TOWN ............ is* permissible, and I/we accept liability for any possible extra cost that may be incurred resulting from such transhipment, and for any loss arising from delay, or from any other cause, due to such transhipment.
   Part shipments xxx are not * permissible.

6. I/We agree that, provided the documents tendered purport to comply with the terms of this Credit, neither the Bank nor its Agents shall be required to investigate their validity, and I/we acquiesce in the acceptance of such documents as relating to goods according to their purport.

7. Failing the fulfilment by me/us of the conditions of this Credit, I/we empower you to land, receive and insure the goods, and sell by public auction or otherwise, as you think fit and proper, the entire shipment for my/our account and risk. In the event of such sale I/we authorise you to retain a commission of 2½% on the gross proceeds after paying the usual commission fees or other charges to Agents, Brokers or others who may be employed by you or for you in the matter, and I/we engage to make good any deficiency on demand.
   *Delete and initial any clauses, etc., inapplicable. [SEE OVER.

114

_Further instructions to bank (or exporter)_

68. A certificate of inspection from our agents, Messrs. . . . must also be produced by the sellers before the draft is honoured.

69. Please open a credit of £2,000 in favour of the Atlantic Trading Co., available to them at 30 d/s in respect of 3 shipments of leather goods as specified on the attached sheet. The beneficiaries are to draw on you for each shipment as these are effected, and the documents required are bills of lading (2), commercial invoices (5), insurance policy, consular invoice and certificate of origin in respect of each shipment.

70. Kindly see that the insurance policy gives the full cover asked for in our letter, before accepting the draft.

71. The forwarding agent's receipt will be acceptable as evidence of shipment in this case and payment may be made on production of this document by the beneficiary.

72. It will be in order to extend the validity of the L/C until 31 December.

73. As we have placed a further order with our suppliers will you please increase the credit to £1,250 in accordance with attached instructions.

_Explanation of reference numbers on pages 103–109_

[1] _proviso_: Condition.

[2] _anticipate_: Begin to use.

[3] _time-lag_: Delay; loss of time.

[4] _given our protection_: Honoured on presentation.

[5] _on a consignment basis_: Without fixed prices.

[6] _under advice_: Drawee is to be notified.

[7] _proceeds_: Results of sale; money collected.

## TERMINOLOGY OF DRAFTS

_acceptance_: (1) An accepted bill; (2) The act of accepting.

_agent_: Any person who acts, under authority, for another person.

_beneficiary_: The person benefiting by a draft.

_'clean' B/E_: A bill of exchange without documents.

_'clean' B/L_: A bill of lading for goods in good condition (see Chapter 8).

_commission_: A charge made on a percentage basis for services.

_copies_: Reproductions of a document.

_correspondent_: Sometimes this term is used for a bank which acts as an agent for another bank.

_days of grace_: 3 days extra in which to settle a time bill.

_defaulter_: A person who fails to pay a debt.

_documentary draft_: A B/E attached to shipping documents.

_domiciliation_: The depositing of a bill by a drawee with a bank for payment when due (_v._ to domicile).

_drawer/ee_: A drawer is the person who draws a bill; a drawee is the person drawn upon.

_due date_: The date by which a bill must be paid.

_dues_: Another word for money due for services.

_endorse (to)_: To sign a document (cheque, bill) passing rights in it to another person.

*evidence (to)*: To prove; to show proof.

*expire (to)*: To come to an end; to be no longer valid.

*extend (to)*: To make a document valid for a longer period.

*honour (to)*: (1) To pay a bill when due; (2) To fulfil an obligation or meet a liability (*neg.* dishonour).

*indemnify (to)*: To compensate a person or free him from liability.

*irrevocable credit*: A credit which cannot be cancelled.

*letter of hypothecation*: A letter given by an exporter to a bank when money is lent against goods shipped; it gives the bank a right of possession of the goods in an emergency.

*negotiate (to)*: To sell, or to discount a bill.

*payer/ee*: payer—one who pays; *payee*—one who receives.

*present (to)*: To send a B/E to the drawee for payment. (*Note: re-present*—to present again; do not confuse with *represent*); (*n.*) presentation.

*proceeds*: The money received from a sale (*Note*: plural only).

*prosecute (to)*: To take legal action against a person when law is transgressed.

*protection*: ('Give our bill your protection') = Please pay when due.

*protest (to)*: To notify publicly the non-payment of a B/E so that legal action may be taken.

*re-imburse (to)*: To pay back money spent by a person on one's behalf.

*remit (to)*: To send money.

*renew (to)*: To issue again; extend; make valid again.

*security*: Documents or valuables given as cover for loan.

*stamp duty*: Tax payable on certain documents (U.K.).

*sue (to)*: To take legal action for non-payment.

*surrender (to)*: To hand over, or give up, documents.

*traveller's L/C*: L/C on which a traveller may draw.

*valid (adj.)*: Effective; in order; having force (*neg.* invalid; (*n.*) validity).

*'value received'*: Words on a British B/E indicating that goods have been received by drawee for the amount of the bill.


## EXERCISES

1. Write a letter for an overseas importer of hardware, in which you order goods from a British manufacturer's catalogue. Say how you wish to pay, as your firm has not yet done business with the seller.

2. Send a letter to a firm in an English-speaking country asking them to supply you with goods on better terms of payment. At present you are accepting drafts at 30 days.

3. You are asked by your employers, a Swiss export company, to write a letter to a British buyer who complains that he does not want to pay against bills drawn in Swiss francs. Offer the buyer either (*a*) sterling

prices, or (*b*) payment by letter of credit payable in Zurich for each order at an agreed rate of exchange.

4. An overseas firm has asked you to supply them with goods to the value of £450. They suggest that you draw on them at 60 d/s for the amount of your invoice. Write a tactful letter explaining that you can only do this against an irrevocable letter of credit confirmed by your bank.

5. A foreign customer has been buying from your firm for a year and has honoured your sight drafts on presentation. He now asks for open account terms with quarterly settlement by B/E. Write two letters, one agreeing to his request and one asking for an irrevocable letter of credit covering the amount of his quarterly requirements.

6. Answer an enquiry from a British firm who want to know what methods of payment your firm are prepared to accept.

7. A foreign supplier has drawn a 60 days' bill on you through your bank, and has failed to notify you of the draft, although you had warned him that you would not accept drafts without advice. Write giving your bank suitable instructions, and also send a letter to the drawer of the bill.

8. Send a letter to a British bank enclosing an acceptance from a British importer, and asking the bank to make certain payments to British firms on your behalf against this acceptance.

9. Write to your bank manager asking him to advance 70% of the value of a consignment of goods you have just exported to a foreign customer.

10. Send a letter to your firm's bank, enclosing shipping documents and a 90 d/s draft on your foreign customer. Ask them to obtain acceptance and then to discount the bill.

11. Your firm's representative in an English-speaking country has sent you an order and advises you that payment will be by irrevocable L/C. Reply to the customer. Write also the customer's letter confirming the order and making payment arrangements.

12. Your bank informs you that a 60 d/s bill drawn by you on a foreign customer has been dishonoured without any explanation. Write to the customer, and also give your bank instructions.

# 10 | Insurance

Insurance has become more and more important as commerce has developed. The idea of insurance is to obtain *indemnity* in the event of any happening that may cause loss of money; insurance is *against risk*. Dancers, for example, may insure their legs, singers their voices, and musicians their hands: indeed, these days it is possible to insure against almost any eventuality that may cause loss of one kind or another.

A somewhat different kind of insurance provides for money to be paid to a person at a certain age as an income or as a lump sum, or to be paid to the person's heirs on his or her death: this is life insurance, now generally known in Britain as *assurance*.

It is not possible in this book to go into the various forms of insurance for private individuals, and we will concern ourselves only with the insurance of goods.

Goods are normally insured for the full amount of their value, which is calculated as: cost of goods + amount of freight + insurance premium + a percentage of the total sum to represent a reasonable profit for the seller.

While goods are being stored—in a warehouse, for example—the insurance usually covers the risks of fire and burglary, and other risks may also be covered. As soon as the goods are *in transit*, in other words being moved from one place to another, they are insured against the same risks. The term *warehoused or in transit* means that the goods are insured whether they are in a warehouse or in process of being moved.

The usual procedure is to insure *against all risks*. This involves a *W.A. clause* (*with average clause*, explained below).

The word *average* as used in insurance means *damage* (it is derived from the French word *avarie*). *With average* means that the insurers pay claims for partial losses, whereas *free of particular average* (F.P.A.) means that partial losses are not covered by the insurance.

*Particular average* means partial loss or damage accidentally caused to the ship or to a particular lot of goods. Particular average must be borne by the owners of the property suffering the loss, and is distinct from general average, which is distributed over the whole ship, freight and cargo. If, for example, some of the cased cycles, the subject of letter no. 1, Chapter 8, become corroded by sea-water a particular average loss has occurred.

*General average* means any extraordinary loss, damage or expenditure incurred for the purpose of preserving all the interests imperilled—the ship, the cargo and the freight: these are said to form a *common adventure*. A general average sacrifice is when cargo has to be *jettisoned*, that

118

means thrown into the sea, to lighten the ship; when cargo is damaged by water used to put out a fire; the cost of towing a ship into port for repair, etc. General average is, in fact, the application of the principle: 'that which is sacrificed for all is borne in proportion by all interested in the adventure'. It is older than insurance.

*The York-Antwerp Rules*: In earlier times there was some conflict between the law of one maritime country and another concerning general average, so a code was drawn up called the York-Antwerp Rules, and this is amended from time to time.

## INSURERS

*Insurers* is the name given to the people who undertake to indemnify the *insured*—that is to say the owners of the goods, whether sellers or buyers, who pay what is called a *premium* to the insurers.

The insurers are also called *underwriters*, and are said *to underwrite* the proportion of the indemnification they are prepared to bear. (The word originated with the insurer's signature under—now usually beside—the proportion he agreed to pay.)

The insurers are either companies, like other business firms, or they belong to the famous organisation of LLOYD'S. This is a very old society that started in London in the eighteenth century; the members operate as individuals and their liability cannot be limited. (*See page 124 for the history of Lloyd's.*)

## DOCUMENTS USED IN INSURANCE

*The policy* is the principal document and is the instrument embodying the contract, but as the policy may cover a certain period of time, or many shipments of goods, another document is used called the *certificate*. This is issued for each shipment that is made, the particulars of the consignment are entered on a *declaration form* and the insurance agents issue the certificate to the senders on behalf of the insurers.

The policy may be known as a *floating policy*, that is to say, it covers a large quantity of goods for a fairly long period, usually a year, or it covers goods up to a large sum of money, and such a policy is represented by certificates for each separate consignment.

There is also a procedure of insurance often used now, known as *open cover*, by which there is a rather general arrangement between the insurer and the insured, that the latter will have all consignments insured by the former.

A *cover note* is a small document issued by the insurance agents to their customers, to tell them that their goods are insured, and to give proof of this until the policy is ready.

The *premium* is the name given to the sum of money paid by the firm insuring its goods, and it is quoted as a percentage. In Britain the rate is quoted as so many pence for every £100 value: 25p% is 25p premium for £100 of merchandise covered. As an example, to insure furniture (against an ordinary fire risk) the quotation % of value is 25p, but for items which are more easily damaged or stolen, such as cameras and jewellery, it is £1%.

## OVERSEAS TRANSPORT

### By rail
British Rail will see to the insurance of the consignments, whether carried by their train-ferries or by train and B.R. vessel; the consignors can deal direct with the railway authority as they would with shipping and forwarding agents, who will also see to all insurance formalities.

The senders endorse the consignment notes at the time of forwarding with the words 'Insurance required for £. . .', an amount which should represent, as nearly as possible, the gross value of the goods.

The insurances provide cover against all risks and every risk and all damage or loss, however caused, but excluding delay and inherent vice* of the goods, at an inclusive premium.

*War risk* is always an extra to the ordinary *all risks* policies.

### By air
Here again the air transport organisations and in particular the State corporations, such as British Airways, will undertake to arrange insurance for consignors. This is indicated on the British Airways contract form. The consignment is insured under an open policy against all risks of physical loss or damage, but again excepting those of war risks, etc.

Generally speaking, insurance for all these different forms of transport is the business of the same insurance companies and Lloyd's. In fact the airlines effect insurance with marine insurance underwriters, and individual shippers can cover their consignments independently in the same way.

### By sea
Here the most complicated form of insurance comes into operation. This is called *marine insurance*, which covers ships and their cargoes.

*Marine insurance* is very old and in the course of time has collected some rather strange terminology and a large number of conditions.

---

* See Chapter 8, page 98.

# CORRESPONDENCE

The senders of the shipment of cycles from London to Malta mentioned in Chapter 8 (letters 1, 3, 5 and 6) would write to their insurance agents and ask for a *rate of insurance*—that is to say, the premium they will have to pay.

## [1] *Enquiry for insurance rate*

Dear Sirs

Please quote us a rate for the insurance against all risks, warehouse to warehouse, of a shipment of

6 (six) cases of cycles, London to Valetta, by *M.V. Morecombe* of the Blue Crescent Line. The value is £. . .

The insurance is needed as from 15 April.

Yours faithfully

When they have been informed of the rate, the senders will instruct the insurance agents to *effect insurance*. If the senders have a floating policy the basic rates will probably have been agreed and they need not ask for a rate, unless special circumstances are involved.

## [2] *Senders' instructions to insurance agents to effect insurance*

We confirm our telegram of today, a copy of which is enclosed, and would be glad if you would cover us against all risks, warehouse to warehouse, to the value of £. . ., on

12 (twelve) cased cycles, London–Malta, by *M.V. Morecombe* of the Blue Crescent Line.

The certificate must reach us by the 17th at the latest, since it has to be presented with the other documents to the bank with which a letter of credit has been opened.

We look forward to your early acknowledgement.

### *Instructions to insurance agents*

1. Please (insure for us) (insure us on) the following: . . .
2. Please (cover for us) (cover us on) the goods detailed below: . . .
3. Please hold us covered (for) (on) the cargo listed on the attached sheet.
4. The goods are lying at 3 Shed, Royal Docks, London, for shipment to Hamburg (by *M.V. Mercury*, . . . Line) (by first available vessel to Hamburg).
5. The cargo is to be insured (warehouse to warehouse) (warehoused or in transit) (against all risks).
6. This consignment is to be covered under our open cover terms.
7. We wish to renew our floating policy no. 56879 on the same terms as before, to cover consignments of textile machinery to West African ports. At the same time please let us have a supply of declaration forms.
8. We shall have several shipments of cement over the next 6 months to West African ports and shall be glad to know your lowest rates F.P.A. The average quantity of each shipment will be about . . . tons, valued . . .
9. We enclose two declaration forms, duly completed, for shipments of general merchandise to Sydney and Melbourne respectively. As this will nearly exhaust the amount of the cover under our policy no. 97539 we shall be glad if you will renew this for a further £10,000.

10. We leave the insurance arrangements to you but we wish to have the goods covered against all risks. The premium is to be charged to the consignees, together with all expenses of forwarding, and will be paid by them on presentation of the documents by your agents in . . .

## Replies from insurance agents

11. We thank you for your instructions to arrange the shipment of . . . We take it that you wish us to insure this cargo against the usual risks, for the value of the goods plus freight. Unless we hear from you to the contrary we shall arrange this.
12. We will effect insurance against all risks, as requested, charging premium and freight to the consignees.
13. We note that you wish to renew the floating policy no. 56879 W.A. covering textile machinery to West African ports, on the same terms; we presume you wish again to have cover up to £15,000.
14. We thank you for your enquiry concerning the shipment of several consignments of cement to West African ports, for which we can quote you as follows: . . . We presume the cement will be packed in stout paper bags.
15. Owing to the fact that these bags have occasionally been dropped into the water during loading and unloading, the insurers have raised the premium to . . .%. We are therefore of the opinion that it would be to your advantage to have W.A. cover instead of F.P.A. The rate for W.A. would be . . .%.

# INSURANCE CLAIMS

As soon as the consignees receive delivery of the consignment, or collect it from the port, airport or goods station agreed on, they must inspect the goods; this should be done without delay, otherwise their claim on the insurers may be jeopardised. However, it is not enough for the buyers to inspect the goods, if damage is discovered; the insurance companies and Lloyd's will not pay compensation unless they receive a report on the damage from a properly qualified and disinterested person. Such a person is called an *insurance surveyor*, and in large centres there are, of course, several surveyors. If the surveyor is employed by Lloyd's then he is a *Lloyd's surveyor*.

The receivers of the goods call in the surveyor to inspect the packing— cases, crates, casks, etc.—and the contents, and to report on the nature and extent of the damage. If the insurance companies and Lloyd's did not require such a report they would soon be out of business, because it would be very easy for buyers to say that the goods had arrived damaged and then put in a claim for compensation.

The buyers also report the damage to the sellers. If, as is probably the case, they are not able to sell the damaged goods, they usually ask for *replacements*. For these they will have to pay separately, setting the amount of the indemnification against this additional payment to be made. In some cases they may be able to sell the goods at a considerably reduced price, as, for example, if the articles have been scratched or chipped; if materials have been spoiled by sea water, fresh water, oil or other stains, part of the material can, perhaps, be cut off and the rest sold.

The letter written to the senders of the consignment will be on the following lines:

## [3] *From consignees to senders, reporting damage*

Dear Sirs

When the *S.S. Elinor Ferguson* arrived at Port-of-Spain yesterday the ship's agents noticed that case no. 14 was damaged, and notified us accordingly. We immediately had the case opened and examined by Lloyd's agent here.

The number of articles in the case tallies with the packing list, but the following are broken:

(list of broken articles)

We enclose copies of the report of the survey and of a declaration by the ship's agents to the effect that the damage was noticed when the case was unloaded.

As you hold the policy, we would be obliged if you would kindly take the matter up with the underwriters, on our behalf; the number of the insurance certificate is, as you know, 3775 842.

In the meantime we will be glad if you will send us replacements for the broken articles as soon as possible, as we have to complete deliveries to our own customers.

We hope to hear from you shortly.

Yours faithfully

*Note* two points in connection with the above letter:
1. Was the bill of lading clean? If so, the shipowners accepted the case as 'in good condition', or as 'in apparent good condition', and are therefore liable; if they contend that the damage was owing to insufficiently strong packing, they should have claused the B/L to that effect when they accepted the consignment for shipment. It is, however, possible that the surveyor may report that the articles were badly packed, which would not be apparent from an outside inspection of the cases, so that the shipowners may claim the damage was due to negligence and not to any fault of theirs.
2. The sale must have been on C.I.F. terms, and the sellers arranged the insurance, sending a certificate to the buyers. As the insurance is evidently of the type known as floating the sellers will continue to hold the policy, which must be produced to the insurers when a claim is made, as the amount of the claim is endorsed on the policy.
   If the sale had been F.O.B. or C. & F. the buyers would have arranged insurance themselves, and the letter would be differently worded at the end, probably as follows:
   *Alternative fourth paragraph for letter no. 3:*
   'We are making a claim on our insurance company and will let you know the result in due course.'

123

*Paragraphs for reports concerning accidents involving the principle of general average*

16. In heavy weather off the coast of France the vessel's rudder was damaged and she was rendered helpless, having in consequence to be towed into Bordeaux, where repairs are now being undertaken. The expenditure thus incurred will be payable by the ship, freight and cargo in proportion to their respective value, and we, as average adjusters,[1] have been appointed to prepare the necessary adjustment.

17. During discharge from the vessel it was noticed that several bales were very damp and badly water-stained. We attribute this to water used to extinguish a fire that broke out in a hold of the vessel, when there was a forced discharge of cargo from that hold.

## LLOYD'S

This is the name of the greatest insurance organisation in the world, but it acquired this name in a rather unusual way; Mr Edward Lloyd kept a coffee house in the City of London, in the eighteenth century, and there the *underwriters* used to meet because it was a good centre for news concerning ships. Later in the same century, after several changes of home, the underwriters occupied the third building of the Royal Exchange (earlier buildings having been destroyed by fire), and organised their business under a Committee of their members. In 1928 they moved to a big new building in Leadenhall Street, and as this soon became too small an extension was built and opened in 1958.

*The Underwriting Room at Lloyd's*

[1] An *average adjuster* is an authority on all aspects of marine insurance law and loss adjustments; he is the expert who assesses the losses and contributions under a general average act. He is a kind of umpire or referee.

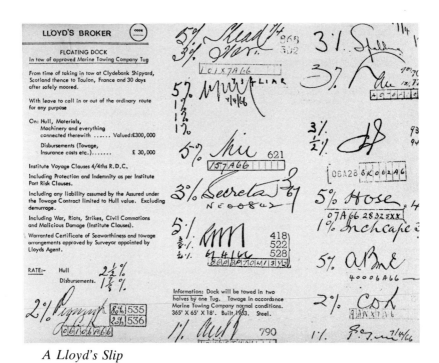

*A Lloyd's Slip*

Lloyd's is not an insurance company or corporation; the members work as individuals, though usually in syndicates. To become a Lloyd's underwriter it is necessary to be approved by the Committee and to pay a very large sum as entrance fee as well as an annual subscription. Lloyd's underwriters are not allowed limited liability, but in the rare cases of failure (as also in the London Stock Exchange) the insured are not allowed to suffer and the Committee pays the outstanding claims.

As the result of the marine insurance business, Lloyd's branched out into shipping intelligence, and *Lloyd's List* is published every day, giving the movements of ships and information of 'casualties'. *Lloyd's Register*, published every year, contains information regarding ships themselves: age, nationality, owners, build, tonnage and classification of all ships surveyed by Lloyd's and conforming to its rules. The classification 'A1-100 Lloyd's' is a guarantee to any prospective purchaser or charterer that the vessel is in good condition and thoroughly seaworthy.

## LIST OF INSURANCE TERMS

*adjuster; adjustment; to adjust.*
*assessor; to assess damage.*
*claim; to claim; to make a claim; to put in a claim.*
*compensation; to compensate.*

*cover; coverage; to cover; to hold covered.*
*damaged (for goods).*
*indemnity; to indemnify.*
*injured (for persons and animals).*
*insurance; insurers; insured; to insure; to effect insurance.*
*loss; to lose.*
*premium; rate of premium; rate of insurance.*
*renewal; renewable; to renew.*
*replacement; to replace.*
*risk; to risk.*
*survey; surveyor; to survey; to make a survey.*

## EXERCISES

1. Fill in the missing words:

   Goods are insured _____ certain risks. They are normally _____ for the full _____ of their _____. If they are found _____ arrival _____ the port _____ destination to be _____, a claim for _____ will be made.

   Details of the agreement between the client and the insurance _____ are to be found in the _____, where the _____ to be paid _____ the client is also mentioned.

   When a Lloyd's agent _____ a damaged consignment, he will also look at the _____ of _____ signed by the captain of the ship. If the _____ of _____ is _____, the captain has _____ the consignment as being in good _____, and so the shipowners may be _____ for the cost of the damaged goods.

2. Write a letter to insurance agents, telling them you have a cargo of machinery for shipment from Liverpool to a South American port, and asking them to arrange insurance.
3. Show in a letter how you would deal with the matter of the renewal of a floating policy.
4. Write a letter from insurance agents, in which they say that the premium on certain goods to a certain destination (which you specify) has been increased; say why this has been done.
5. Write to your insurance agents, pointing out that as special packing is now used for certain goods, you think that the insurance rate could be lower.
   As the insurance agents, reply to this letter.
6. Notify your suppliers of certain damage to a consignment received and say what action has been taken.

# 11 | Complaints and replies to complaints

Ideally, it should not be necessary to complain, since in business every-thing should be done so carefully—details of offers and orders checked, packing supervised, quality control carried out expertly—that no mis-takes are made and nothing is damaged. Unfortunately, as in other walks of life,[1] things do not work out as well as that. Errors occur and goods are mishandled; accidents happen, usually because of haste and lack of supervision. There is often a shortage of staff owing to illness or holidays, and there is sometimes a shortage of sufficiently trained staff, so mistakes are inevitable and customers complain.

It should be a point of honour[2] with a firm never to blame its employees when writing replies to complaints: the firm has undertaken the work and the staff are part of the firm, therefore the firm itself is at fault and must take the consequences.

Complaints may be of several kinds, and may arise from the delivery of wrong goods, damaged goods, or too many or too few goods. Even if the right articles are delivered in the right quantities, they may arrive later than expected, thus causing severe difficulty to the buyer and, possibly, to his customers. Then the quality of the goods may be unsatisfactory: perhaps they are not according to the sample or description on the basis of which they were ordered, or they may simply be second-rate products.

If a customer is dissatisfied with the execution of his order, he will complain. In doing so he should refer clearly to the articles in question, by referring to his own order number or to that of his supplier's invoice, or both. He should then specify the nature of his complaint, and finally state what action he wants his supplier to take.

Here are some examples of letters of complaint written by customers to their suppliers:

[1] *Complaint of late delivery*

Dear Sirs

Our order no. VF449766 of 4 July 1978

The goods ordered under this number arrived today in good condition, and your invoice has been checked and found correct.

However, we have to point out that these articles were ordered subject to their arriving here by the end of August. Since they did not reach us until 14 September, we have been hard pressed to meet our commitments to our own customers.

As you will no doubt understand, a recurrence of this situation could well result in our customers placing orders elsewhere, and this is a risk we are unwilling to take. We must, therefore, insist that you observe delivery deadlines for future orders.

Yours faithfully

## [2] *Customer complains of repeated delays in delivery*

Dear Sirs

Our order nos. 6531, 6687, 6866 and 6892

As we have repeatedly pointed out to you, prompt delivery on your part is essential if we are to maintain satisfactory stock levels and fulfil our production schedules.

Each of the four orders listed above has arrived later than the date stipulated, and order no. 6892 was delayed by almost a month, with the result that we have had to reduce production by some 5 per cent.

We cannot possibly allow this situation to continue, and are sorry to have to tell you that unless you can guarantee to deliver supplies by the dates specified in future orders, we will be forced to look for another supplier.

We hope to hear from you very soon.

Yours faithfully

## [3] *Customer receives wrong goods*

Dear Sirs

Our order no. J733

We have received the documents[3] and taken delivery of the goods which arrived at Port Elizabeth on the *S.S. Castle* yesterday.

We are much obliged to you for the prompt execution of this order. Everything seems to be correct and in good condition except in case no. 14.

Unfortunately, when we opened this case we found it contained completely different articles from those ordered, and we can only presume that a mistake has been made and that this case is part of another order.

As we need the articles we ordered to complete deliveries to our customers, we must ask you to arrange for replacements to be despatched at once. We attach a list of the contents of case 14, and would be glad if you would check this against our order and your copy of the invoice. In the meantime we are holding the case at your disposal;[4] please let us know what you wish us to do with it.

Yours faithfully

## [4] *Complaint of inferior quality*

Dear Sirs

We are very sorry to have to inform you that your last delivery is not up to your usual standard. The material seems to be too loosely woven and is inclined to pull out of shape. By separate mail we have sent you a cutting from this material, also one from cloth of an early consignment, so that you can compare the two and see the difference in texture.

We have always been able to rely on the high quality of the materials you sent us and we are all the more disappointed in this case because we supplied the cloth to new customers. As we shall have to take it back we must ask you to let us know, without delay, what you can do to help us in getting over this difficulty.

Yours faithfully

Here is a list of sentences which may be used in various types of complaints:

## Poor quality goods, wrong goods

1. You have supplied goods below the standard we expected from the samples.
2. The bulk of the goods delivered is not up to sample.
3. The goods we have received do not tally with the sample on which we ordered.
4. Unfortunately, we find you have sent us the wrong goods.
5. On comparing the goods received with the sample, we were surprised to find that the colour is not the same.
6. Evidently some mistake was made and the goods have been wrongly delivered.
7. The finish is not good and the enamel has cracked in some places.
8. The heads of the screws should have been below the outer surface, whereas they stand out above it.
9. The chromium finish is not so bright as it should be and in some places is discoloured.
10. The pattern is uneven in places and the colouring varies.
11. We cannot possibly supply our customers with the articles we have received from you.
12. Our chemist reports that the content is not up to the (percentage) (proportion) agreed.
13. We have had an analysis made and the analyst reports (that the chemical content is . . .% deficient in . . .).
14. We cannot accept these containers as they are not the size and shape we ordered.
15. We find that you have sent us an article marked DC/56 instead of the BC/56 we ordered; we take it that this was due to a typist's error, but as the articles sent are not of the type we stock, we must ask for replacement by the correct number as soon as possible.

## Missing from the delivery

16. On checking the goods received we find that several items on your invoice have not been included; we enclose a list of the missing articles.
17. Unfortunately you have not sent us all the goods we ordered; the following are missing: . . .
18. There is a discrepancy between the packing list of case 52 and your invoice: 3 dozen tea services are correctly entered on the invoice but there were only 2 dozen in the case.
19. We regret to have to tell you that case 20 contains only 10 plastic bowls instead of 12 entered on the packing list and also on the invoice. The case shows no signs of pilferage and we shall be glad if you will check up with your packers before we make a claim.
20. You have short-shipped this consignment by 100 kg.

The buyers need not accept any goods received that are not in accordance with their order, except as the result of alterations made by agreement with the sellers, but they may make an offer to keep the goods at a reduced price.

The buyers are entitled to return to the sellers any goods received that they did not order, but in the export trade it is usual for the buyers first to find out what the sellers' wishes are in the matter. This is a question of courtesy and consideration, as the reimportation of goods into a country will involve Customs entries and other formalities, to say nothing of[5] the actual cost of freight and insurance. It is also possible that the wrongly delivered goods may have been intended for another customer in the same country as the receivers, and so the goods can be sent on to the correct address. It is better if the sellers instruct their own shipping and forwarding agents to attend to this, through their branch or correspondents in the country of the buyers, rather than involve the latter in the trouble of sending on goods.

(*Note* the fourth paragraph of letter no. 7.)

## Offer to keep goods at a reduced price

21. Although the quality of these goods is not up to that of our usual lines we are prepared to accept them if you will reduce the price, say,[6] by . . .
22. We are only prepared to accept the goods sent if you are willing to make a substantial reduction in the price.


## Complaint of delay

23. When we sent you our order we pointed out (that prompt delivery was most essential) (that early delivery of the goods was absolutely necessary).
24. We urged on you the importance of the time factor.
25. The delivery time was clearly stated on our order and your (acknowledgement) (acceptance).
26. In your acknowledgement of our order you stated that the consignment would be despatched within (two weeks) (a fortnight) and we are therefore very surprised that we have had no advice of despatch yet.
27. We are at a loss to understand[7] why we have not heard from you.
28. We are still without your advice of despatch of the cameras; we are receiving urgent requests from customers and you will understand that this delay places us in an awkward position.
29. As you know from our previous correspondence, these goods represent a considerable part of a big order, and it is absolutely essential that the delivery should be punctual, otherwise the installation of the machinery cannot be carried out by the date agreed.
30. You will remember that it was agreed the goods would be shipped in time to arrive here by the end of the month.
31. If the goods have not yet been shipped we must ask you to send them by air.
32. Our stocks may become too low for us to be able to cope with the Christmas trade.
33. An explanation of this delay will be appreciated.
34. We must ask you to despatch the consignment immediately, if you have not already done so, and in any case please inform us by cable what the position is.
35. We hope to hear from you by return that the consignment is on its way.
36. We have asked our bank for information but they say they have not received any documents from you yet.
37. Any delay now will cause us a loss of business.
38. Although we have had no news from you since your letter of the 5th of last month, we have no doubt that you did ship the goods on the 24th as agreed, but, owing to your failure to keep us informed, we have not been able to obtain insurance cover and the goods are therefore being carried at your risk.
39. Our import licence is due to expire on the 30th of this month, and if there is any delay in renewing it the consignment may have to be held up[8] at the docks, which will add to the cost of the shipment and cause great inconvenience. We therefore urge you to do everything possible to hasten the despatch.

## Bad packing

40. We regret that we have to complain about the way in which the consignment just received has been packed.
41. The packing inside the case (was too loose) (was insufficient) with the result that there was some shifting of the contents and several cups and plates have been broken. The attached list will give you details.
42. Some of the polythene bags seem to have burst, either as the result of chemical action of the contents or because the polythene is not thick enough. It would be advisable to have tests made to discover the cause of the breaking.
43. The seams of the jute sacks do not appear to have been strong enough, with the result that they have given way,[9] thus allowing the contents to run out.
44. The adhesive tape seems to have dried in some cases, so that the lids became loose. We would therefore advise you to see whether the tape used was defective in any way.
45. The cartons appear to have been very roughly handled at some time during loading or discharging, but fortunately the metal bands held firm and the contents have not suffered any damage.
46. One of the parts in case no. 69 came adrift[10] and has been dented, in consequence of contact with the other parts. We believe we can have the dent pressed out, but this may affect the selling price and in that case we must reserve the right to call on you for compensation.
47. We have had the case and contents examined by the insurance surveyor but, as you will see from the enclosed copy of his report, he maintains that the damage was probably due to insecure packing and not to any unduly rough handling of the case.

## Warnings of cancellation, etc.

Warnings and threats should not be used too liberally, or they will only create bad feeling and in many cases would be quite unnecessary, even unwise. However, if there are constant or needlessly prolonged delays, or frequent mistakes in carrying out orders, the buyers may be obliged to write in this way. The following are the usual phrases in English writing.

48. We must ask you to carry out our orders more carefully in future.
49. We must insist on more careful (execution of our orders) (attention being given to our instructions).
50. We regret that unless we hear from you by return we shall be obliged (to cancel the order) (to terminate the agreement).
51. We shall be (forced) (compelled) to hand the matter over to our solicitors.
52. We are very reluctant (to take this step) (to take such action) and we hope it will not be necessary.
53. We trust you will not make it necessary for us (to do this) (to take legal action) (to take such a step).

## REPLIES TO COMPLAINTS

These should always be courteous; even if the sellers think that the complaint is unfounded they should not say so until they have good and reliable grounds on which to repudiate the claim. All complaints should be treated as serious matters and thoroughly investigated.

If the sellers are the first to discover that a mistake has been made they should not wait for a complaint, but should write, cable or telephone at once to let the buyers know, and either put the matter right or offer some compensation.

On receiving the complaint the sellers will make investigations, and if the complaint is justified they will at once apologise to the buyers and suggest a solution. If the buyers have offered to keep the goods, the sellers will probably agree to this and to a price reduction. The amount of the reduction will depend on how bad the mistake is, and in some cases a substantial reduction, even with consequent loss, is of more advantage to the sellers than the expense and trouble of having the goods returned to them, and of causing inconvenience to their customers. However, if the value of the goods in question is high, it may be advisable to have them returned, although even in this case the added risk of damage in further transport may not be worth incurring.

There is no need for the sellers to go into a long story of how the mistake was made. A short explanation may be useful but, generally speaking, the buyers are not interested in hearing how or why the error occurred but only in having the matter put right, in receiving the goods they ordered—or at least value for the money they have paid—or in knowing when they may expect to receive the delayed consignment.

In *no* case should the sellers blame their staff; their sole aim is to put the trouble right and restore good relations with their customers.

## [5] *Supplier's reply to letter no. 1*

Dear Sirs

Thank you for your letter of 17 September. We are pleased to hear that the goods ordered under your no. VF449766 arrived in good condition, but must apologise for their delayed arrival.

We have looked into the matter, and have found that the delay is due to a minor fault in one of our routines, which has now been rectified. We can assure you that future orders from you will be dealt with promptly, and that consignments will reach you by the dates stipulated.

Once again, please accept our apologies for this delay.

Yours faithfully

## [6] *Reply to letter no. 2*

Dear Sirs

Your letter of 6 October 1978: your order nos. 6531, 6687, 6866 and 6892

We have received your letter, and must ask you to accept our apologies for despatching these orders later than the scheduled dates.

As we informed you in our letter of 8 August, there was some disagreement between management and the trade union in the latter part of the summer, and this resulted in greatly reduced production at two of our plants in the north of England. It was at this time that we introduced electronic data processing of orders here at head office, and, like most other companies, we had one or two problems to sort out in the early stages.

However, these difficulties have now been cleared up, and our production is now running according to plan. We are, naturally, very sorry for the inconvenience you have had to suffer on account of our own problems, but we can promise you that you can rely on prompt delivery on our part now that the situation is back to normal.

Yours faithfully

## [7] *Supplier's reply to letter no. 3*

Dear Sirs

Your order no. J733. Your letter OG/MR of 11 October 1977

Thank you for your letter. We are pleased to hear that the consignment was delivered promptly, but are very sorry to learn that case no. 14 did not contain the goods you ordered.

On going into the matter we find that a mistake was made in the packing, through a confusion of numbers, and we have arranged for the right goods to be despatched to you at once. The documents will be mailed to you within the next forty-eight hours.

We have already cabled you in this connection, and enclose a copy of the telegram.

We would be grateful if you would kindly keep case no. 14 and its contents until they are called for by the local representatives of World Transport Ltd., our forwarding agents, who we have already instructed.

Please accept our many apologies for the trouble caused to you by the error.

Yours faithfully

## [8] *Exporters' reply to letter no. 4*

Dear Sirs

We have received your letter of 14 October and thank you for sending us the two samples of cloth for examination.

We have passed these on to the factory for comment and we quote the following from their reply:

'It was found that some short-staple yarn[11] had, by accident, been woven into the material, and this cloth was put on one side for disposal in a suitable market. Evidently through an oversight some of the cloth was packed in your consignment. The factory manager was very grateful for the samples, as it is possible other buyers may have received these imperfect goods, and enquiries are being made accordingly.'

We told the manufacturers how greatly concerned we were over your disappointment in the quality, and the fact that you had supplied the cloth to new customers. They expressed their very great regret, and we have arranged with them for the immediate despatch of replacements, *franco domicile*,[12] duty paid. Furthermore, they guarantee the quality of the cloth now sent.

If you care to dispose of the inferior cloth at the best price obtainable for it, we will send you a credit note for the difference as soon as we hear from you.

We apologise sincerely for the trouble caused to you, and will take all possible steps to ensure that such a mistake is not made again.

Yours faithfully

In the case of letter no. 8, the sellers might not admit any fault in the cloth, and among the following sentences are some that they could use:

## Replies to complaints of poor quality

54. We were very sorry to receive your complaint that the material you received was not of the quality expected.
55. We have been supplying the same material for some time past and have had no complaints about it so far.
56. The defect may be due to a fault in a machine and we are having a check-up made on all the (machines) (looms).
57. The samples you sent us are not large enough to judge by and we shall be much obliged if you will return us the whole piece. The cost of returning will, of course, be borne by us.
58. We think the best procedure will be to have the pieces examined by an expert and we are arranging for this to be done.
59. We have asked our shipping agents to collect the case from you, for delivery to the customer to whom it should have been sent.
60. We shall be glad if you will return the goods to us, and we have arranged collection by . . .
61. The (articles) (appliances) were carefully examined in the usual way before being packed and we cannot understand how the enamel came to be cracked. As our Export Manager is paying a visit to your country next month he will call to see you, and we shall be much obliged if you will keep the articles on one side until he can inspect them.
62. We greatly regret the mistake in the number, which resulted in your receiving the wrong articles . . .
63. We were sorry to see from your letter that you expected to receive no. BC/56; on looking at your order again we see that what looked like a 'D' could indeed be 'B', but the typing was smudged and not clear. If you will examine your own copy of the order we think you will see that this is so. Furthermore we stated DC/56 on our acknowledgement and this must have escaped your notice.

## Goods missing from the delivery short-shipped—short-delivered

64. On receiving your letter and list of goods you say were missing from the consignment, we checked up with the packers. It appears that an extra case had to be used to take all the articles of the order, and this case is included on the bill of lading, as you will see if you examine one of the copies.
We would suggest that you make enquiries with the agents in your port.
65. We greatly regret that you received only 2 dozen instead of the 3 dozen ordered. On investigation we find that the packers misread the number, and we have arranged with them for the immediate despatch (of the missing 1 dozen) (of the 1 dozen short-shipped).
66. According to our records the complete dozen were packed and we are afraid that the case must have been opened, although it may show no signs of this. We can send you evidence of the correct shipment, so that you can take the matter up at your end. If you require any action on our part please let us know.
67. On making enquiries concerning the missing drum we have discovered that it was left behind on the quay; the shipping agents inform us, however, that it was put on the next ship, the M.V. . . ., which is due to arrive at your port on 6 February. The local agents have already received advice of this and will communicate with you on the arrival of the vessel.

## Replies to offer to keep goods at a reduced price

68. We appreciate your offer to keep the goods wrongly delivered, and we are ready to allow . . .% off the invoice price. We hope this will meet with your approval.
69. In view of the high quality of the article, we regret that we cannot reduce the price. If you are unable to accept it, we will make arrangements for its collection and (return to us) (delivery to another customer).

## Replies to complaints of delay

70. We received your letter of September 4, and immediately cabled you, as per copy enclosed, stating that the goods were despatched on the 1st, which we confirm.
71. There was a slight delay due to the breakdown of a machine, which held up (production) (packing) for (a day) (a day or two), but as we knew it would not affect the delivery limit we did not notify you.
72. The goods are already on their way and the documents were duly handed to the bank.
73. Our advice of despatch was mailed to you and you will doubtless have received it by now.
74. We regret that you had the trouble of writing to us, and your letter must have crossed with ours advising you of the shipment of the consignment.
75. The factory have advised us that owing to an unexpected demand, they have not been able to cope with orders and are behindhand with some deliveries.
76. We have asked the manufacturers to give your order priority, which they have promised to do.
77. Owing to a lightning strike in the factory the production was held up for twenty-four hours. The strike has been settled but there is likely to be some delay, although the workers are on overtime.
78. We regret that no priority can be given, but you can be sure that all orders are being executed in strict rotation.
79. We are extremely sorry about this delay, which you will realise was due to circumstances beyond our control.

*Note*: All contracts contain clauses exempting suppliers and transport people from any liability due to *strikes* and such actions outside the control of the senders and carriers.

## Replies to complaints of bad packing

80. As soon as we received your letter we got in touch with the packers and asked them to look into the matter.
81. We have passed on your complaint to the firm of packers that handled this consignment, and have asked them to send us a report.
82. We have been in touch with the manufacturers of the bags and have asked them (to strengthen the material) (to reinforce the seams).
83. Our stock of adhesive tape has been carefully examined and it seems to be in very good condition. We can only surmise that the tins were exposed to heat, or the cartons may have been stowed near boilers.
84. The packers do not agree that there is any defect in the material used, and there have been no previous complaints; they maintain that the cases must have (had) (been subjected to) very (rough handling) (rough treatment).
85. We are very pleased to hear that the metal bands held firm, but we will use stouter packing in future.

135

## Replies to warnings of cancellation

86. It was with great regret that we read your final remark, and we sincerely hope you will not consider it necessary to take such a drastic step.

87. We should like to say that we greatly appreciate your patience in this most unfortunate matter, but as we have hopes of getting it cleared up in the very near future we must ask you to do nothing final yet.

88. We feel that your threat of cancellation is unjustified and we shall be obliged to hold you to your contract.

89. As we do not feel we have had the co-operation from you (that we expected) (that we were entitled to), we ourselves are not prepared to continue the contract and will give you due notice of termination.


## LEGAL ACTION

A note here on the taking of *legal action*: no sensible firm does this except on the advice of a lawyer. The language of the law in all countries is inclined to be rather old-fashioned and difficult to understand, but more simple language is often dangerous as it may be differently interpreted; for this reason the actual wording of contracts of any kind should also be subject to the approval of a lawyer. Businessmen prefer to write in a straightforward and simple way, but care must always be taken in writing a letter to a firm in another country. Misinterpretation may lead to legal action.


*Explanation of reference numbers in this chapter*

[1] *other walks of life*: People in different circumstances.

[2] *a point of honour*: A matter of conscience.

[3] *we have received the documents*: The documents are the shipping documents. (*See Chapter 8*)

[4] *we are holding the case at your disposal*: This means that we have not accepted the case and contents, which are still the property of the senders.

[5] *to say nothing of*: Not to mention.

[6] *say, by . . .*: (1) Used, as here, to indicate a suggestion; (2) To indicate a sum of money repeated in words after the figures.

[7] *at a loss to understand*: We cannot find any reason.

[8] *to be held up*: To be delayed.

[9] *have given way*: Have not been able to hold firm and have therefore broken or collapsed.

[10] *came adrift*: Became unfastened (it is derived from boats and ships; 'to cast adrift' is to unfasten the vessel).

[11] *short-staple yarn*: The thread or yarn used in weaving may have a basic short or long length, according to the natural wool; long staple gives the cloth greater strength.

[12] *franco domicile*: (*See the price terms on page 19 of Chapter 3*)

## SOME VOCABULARY OF CHAPTER 11

*awkward (adj.)*: Difficult, inconvenient.

*bulk (n.)*: (1) The goods delivered in a sale by sample; (2) The majority, most of the goods.

*check up (v.)*: To see if everything is all right.

*cope with (v.)*: To manage, but always with some difficulty.

*dispose of (v.)*: (1) To get rid of; (2) To sell.

*finish (n.)*: The completed surface of the article or material.

*item (n.)*: Used only to refer to something *in a list*, in a catalogue.

*line (n.)*: The kind of material or article dealt in or made, the kind of business.

*missing (adj.)*: What is not there but should be.

*pilferage (n.)*: Petty theft.

*replacement (n.)*: In the case of breakage or wrong delivery another consignment of the goods ordered is sent to take the place of the broken, damaged or wrongly delivered goods.

*staff (n.)*: The employees.

*substantial (adj.)*: Big, large.

*take for granted (v.)*: To presume (usually abbreviated to: take it).

*texture (n.)*: Structure of material, thickness, weave of fabric.

*viewpoint (n.)*: Point of view.

## EXERCISES

1. Write a letter from buyers, saying that some articles are missing from a delivery.
2. As the suppliers, reply to the previous letter.
3. As buyers, write to your suppliers and ask them why you have not had any advice from them yet of the despatch of a consignment.
4. Write a letter from buyers in an eastern country, informing suppliers that certain articles they sent have been affected by the heat, in spite of a guarantee that this would not happen; say what you propose in the matter.
5. As exporters, write to your customers advising them about a strike that may delay shipment of their order.
6. Write to your suppliers and inform them that several articles in one case have been broken, owing to insecure packing; the insurance surveyor has reported this.
7. As the exporters, write a tactful letter to customers who have complained that the material they have received is not like the samples on which they gave the order.
8. As suppliers, reply to a complaint of missing goods, asking customers to make a careful check at their end, as everything was correct when the goods were packed and shipped.

# 12 | Agencies

A vast amount of international trade is handled not by direct negotiation between buyer and seller but by agencies, usually in the country of the buyer. Of course, a large organisation may establish a manufacturing subsidiary or sales company in the foreign country it sells to, but this calls for enormous capital outlay and is beyond the means of most exporters. Even for those who can afford to establish branches abroad it may be very questionable whether they would prove economical to run. It is, therefore, not surprising that agencies continue to handle a very large volume of business.

This chapter deals with the correspondence of agencies, and for a better understanding of the letters contained in it, we will refer very briefly to some of the various types of agents.

The *forwarding agent* has already been described in Chapter 8, and this type of agency should be mentioned again here because there is a growing tendency for forwarding agents to extend their activities into the fields of transport, financing, insurance, and even buying on their own account.

*Mercantile agents* may be *selling agents* or *buying agents*; both act on instructions from their *principals*, and receive payment for their services under some kind of agreement or contract. *Brokers* and *factors* are also mercantile agents, but agents with higher degrees of independent authority. Brokers and factors often deal in commodities such as fruit, agricultural produce, and raw materials, whose prices are subject to sudden changes.

*Commission agents* buy and sell in their own names, on the best terms available, on behalf of foreign buyers and sellers. They charge a *commission* for their work.

*Merchant shippers* are import/export merchants who buy and sell entirely in their own right and for their own account, but who may be considered agents in the wider sense of the term.

Their function is rather like that of the wholesaler in the home trade, but they have the additional work of attending to shipping arrangements.

The letters which follow deal less with the routine side of the work of agencies than with particular problems: terms of operation, competition, supplies, and so forth. The more personal and informal style of this correspondence should prove of value to the student, for a good deal of the subject matter and idiom can be applied to matters other than those connected with agencies.

138

## [1] *Importer asks for agency*

L. PETERSEN A.S.

Glostrupgade 154
Copenhagen S

4 January 1978

Modern Garden Implements Ltd.
Wendover Avenue
Birmingham UTT 8FR
England

Dear Sirs

The excellent quality and modern design of your mechanical garden tools, a
selection of which we saw recently in action here, appeals to us very much.
We have since seen your full catalogue and are interested to know whether
you have considered the possibilities of the market in this country.

As a leading firm of importers and distributors of many years' standing in
this trade, we have an extensive sales organisation and a thorough knowledge
of the Danish market. We think your products would sell very well here,
and are prepared to do business with you either on a consignment basis or
by placing firm orders, if your prices and terms are right.

We are also interested in handling a sole agency for you, which we think
would be to our mutual advantage.

Please let us have your views on these proposals: if you are interested
in establishing an agency here, our Mr Eriksen would be pleased to call
on you in March, when he will be in England.

We look forward to your reply.

Yours faithfully

*L. Petersen.*

L. Petersen A.S.

## [2] *Manufacturer replies: answer to letter no. 1*

Dear Sirs

We thank you for your letter of 4 January and are pleased to hear that you find our products satisfactory and that you think there is room for expanded sales in Denmark.

If your Mr Eriksen will call on us when he is in our district we shall be pleased to discuss the possibility of coming to an arrangement with you, but we have not yet made any decision about an agency. Perhaps you would like to give us some idea of the terms on which you would be willing to operate as our agent, and approximately what amount of stock you would wish to hold.

Meanwhile we have pleasure in sending you our export catalogue with full details of discounts, and we should be pleased to supply you with an initial order at these prices against your letter of credit, available by draft on a British bank at 60 days after shipment of the goods.

Yours faithfully

## [3] *Exporter offers agency*

Dear Sirs

In view of the steady increase in the demand for our beauty preparations,[1] we have decided to appoint an agent to handle our export trade with your country.

From our own observations and the experiences of competitors, we are convinced that there is an enormous market potential[2] waiting to be tapped, and a really active, go-ahead[3] agent could develop a fine business in this line. As we think you are the right people to do this, we should like to offer you the agency if you are at all interested, and we should welcome your views.

We offer a sole agency, and would supply you with a reasonable initial[4] stock on a credit of 6 months. Further supplies would be invoiced to you at 10% below export list prices, with payment by quarterly draft.

An early reply would be appreciated, as we wish to reach a quick decision. Meanwhile we hope you will see in our offer a worthwhile[5] opportunity.

Yours faithfully

## [4] *Importer replies to offer: answer to letter no. 3*

We appreciate the confidence you show in us by offering us a sole agency here for your products.

You are right in saying that there is an increasing demand for your class of preparations in our country, although we think it impossible yet to judge the sales level that could be reached. Women here are not so fashion-conscious and it would need an extensive advertising campaign to create a really wide interest. Then you have to face the competition of the big firms with international connections.

However, we are willing to give it a trial if you feel disposed to back us up[6] with a reasonable amount of advertising in the first year. We are sure you will appreciate that our own advertising would be inadequate to meet the needs of getting your lines established, and that we could not be expected to bear these costs.

Your comments will be very welcome, and we thank you meanwhile for giving us the first opportunity of taking up your agency.

140

# [5] *An agency is confirmed*

OFFICE AUTOMATS LTD. LONDON

27 March 1978

Olympus A.G.
Stuttgart.

Dear Sirs

We are pleased to confirm the agreement reached at the recent discussions at Stuttgart between you and our Mr. P. Henry, and look forward very much to a successful co-operation.

Before the contract is drawn up for signature we should like to re-state the main points of the agreement:

1. That we operate as sole agents for a period of three years from date of agreement[7].
2. That we receive a commission of 10% on all sales of your machines in the United Kingdom.
3. That we handle no other imported machines of a competitive type.
4. That we render you monthly account sales[8] and accept your drafts on us for the net amount of these sales.
5. That we maintain a comprehensive range[9] of your products prominently displayed in our main showrooms in Kingsway, London.

We look forward to your letter confirming these points, or your draft agreement[10].

Yours faithfully

# [6] *Foreign agent advises British exporter on prices*

Dear Sir

With reference to your quotation of 2 May, we now have the pleasure of sending you our indent no. 36 for various tablecloths, table-covers and curtain material.

We have had some difficulty in obtaining this order as the prices quoted by you exceed the limits given us by our customer. You will doubtless be aware of the growing competition in this market from Indian and Chinese products, all of which are of quite good quality and considerably cheaper than yours. The pleasing designs of your patterns finally decided our customer to place his order, but we think that you would find a general reduction in prices advisable if you wish to remain competitive.

Please arrange for early shipment and draw on us at 2 months for the amount of your invoice, less our commission and charges as noted.

Yours faithfully

# [7] *Agent asks for increased commission*

Dear Sirs

Your letter describing the new lines you wish to put on the market in this country interests me very much. There is a lively demand for the smaller type of electric household appliances[11] and I am keen[12] to assist you to get your products known here.

However, as you probably know, your American, German and Japanese competitors are very firmly established in this market and it will be a hard fight to win business in the face of[13] such opposition. I am quite willing to step up[14] my advertising and really make a strong sales drive[15] because I am sure that there is business to be obtained. This would mean a considerable capital outlay, from which you would also have lasting benefit, and

141

in view of this I must ask you to bear part of the costs. Perhaps the easiest way would be for you to allow me an increased commission on the sale of these new lines. I shall be pleased to hear what you have to suggest in this direction.

Yours faithfully

## [8] *Export manufacturer's reply to agent: answer to letter no. 7*

Dear Sirs

From your reply to our letter introducing our new lines we gather[16] that you are willing to make an all-out[17] effort to establish them on your market. We are pleased to have this confirmation of our own judgement.

Taking the long view,[18] we think that the sturdy construction of our machines and the very competitive prices will ensure steady and increasing sales in your country, despite the opposition. At the same time we appreciate that some judicious[19] advertising will speed up the sales process and that it is not reasonable to ask you to bear the whole cost of this.

We find it difficult to allow increased commission on our goods, as prices have been finely calculated, but are prepared to grant you a credit of £500 towards initial advertising costs. We think this is a more practical way of meeting the position.

If you decide to accept this offer, please let us know what kind of campaign you would run. Our opinion is that trade papers[20] are the best medium, but we are quite willing to rely on your judgement.

Yours faithfully

## [9] *Import agent rejects export offer*

We thank you for your letter of . . . in which you offer us a range of your goods for re-sale in this country.

Unfortunately, we cannot make use of your offer; we operate as agents only and do not buy on our own account. We must also say that at the prices fixed in your catalogue there would be little hope of finding a market for your goods, especially as they are unknown in this country. In our opinion, rigid price quotations on your side at this stage are not practical.

As, however, the demand here for goods in your line is rising, we think we can do business for you if you are able to set a lower limit on your prices and allow us to handle your goods on a consignment basis. We would then get the best prices for you within the given limits.

If this proposal is acceptable to you please let us know so that we can discuss details.

## [10] *Agent's report and account sales*

Our account sales for the March quarter is enclosed with this letter and shows a balance of £2,100 in your favour. If you will draw on us for this amount at 60 days we will accept the draft on presentation.

We very much regret the fall in sales in the past quarter year, which is undoubtedly due to the new import duties which came into force on 1 January. This is likely to operate with increasing disadvantage to exports from countries outside the tariff wall. No doubt you have plans to meet the strong competition which we will now have to face in this market, and further information from you on this point would be useful to us in respect of our own plans for the future. Some reduction in prices seems inevitable if you wish to hold your position.

For our part, we wish to continue to represent you and are fairly sure that the high reputation of your goods in this country will ensure the continued support of many customers. We are also prepared to accept a 2% reduction in commission If you are prepared to make an all-round price cut.[21]

We look forward to your reply and wish to assure you of increased effort on your behalf.

## [11] *Agent's complaint of slow delivery*

Dear Sirs

We enclose account sales for the past month and will credit you with the amount shown, on receipt of your confirmation of our figures.

You will see that our sales of the special line ordered in our cable of 3 February are disappointing, and we must say that we cannot accept any responsibility for this. Our telegram called for URGENT treatment of the order and we had reckoned on getting the goods within 3 weeks. Actually, 5 weeks went by before the goods arrived and this let our competitors in[22] and lost a wonderful opportunity of getting exceptional prices.

On enquiry we found that the goods were not shipped until 3 weeks after the date of our telegram. If they had been routed via Southampton instead of London a great deal of valuable time would have been saved.

Competition from the East is growing, and apart from lower prices, some of these firms are able to offer quick deliveries. It will therefore be necessary to give us your very best attention if you wish to retain a hold on this market.

Yours faithfully

## [12] *Fruit broker's report to grower*

Account sales for your consignment by *S.S. Windsor Castle* is enclosed with this letter and you will see that we were able to get very good prices for the plums in almost every case. The few markets where we were not able to do so well had already been heavily supplied by competitors, but the total obtained for you is well above market average for the whole consignment.

With regard to the pears, we have been less fortunate. These were not in a fit condition, when unloaded, to send to overseas markets: they were so ripe that we were obliged to dispose of them locally and at rather low prices, to ensure a quick sale. We suggest you claim on the carriers for any loss involved, as we think these pears must have been held up a week at Cape Town. According to your consignment advice no. . . . of 18 January, the fruit should have arrived a week earlier in *S.S. Arundel Castle*.

Fruit prices generally are being maintained and we think you may look forward with confidence to a good season.

## [13] *British buying agent's order to English manufacturer*

Dear Sir

I have just received the following order from a customer in Ghana:

1.  5 dozen tea services, floral pattern
2.  3  ,,  dinner  ,,  ,,  ,,
3.  4 gross cups & saucers, seconds,[23] white

Your catalogue nos. 53 and 65 would be suitable for items (1) and (2) respectively, and if you can guarantee delivery at Liverpool by 15 May latest, you may take this as my official

143

order. I leave item (3) to your discretion, as you have supplied these odd[24] cups and saucers on previous occasions and know the sort of thing required.

Kindly confirm acceptance of the order by return and send advice of despatch together with 3 copies of your invoice to my office at Liverpool Docks.

Yours faithfully

## [14] *Buying agent rejects order*
Dear Sirs

Many thanks for your indent no. 107 of 1 March.

We regret having to refuse this, but the delivery date stipulated[25] by you does not give us sufficient time in which to obtain most of the items required. The minimum period necessary where goods have to be obtained from Switzerland or Germany is 4–5 weeks.

We are anxious to serve you but are sure you will see the need for giving us a little more notice[26] of your requirements.

Yours faithfully

*Explanation of reference numbers in letters 1–14*
[1] *beauty preparations*: Shampoo, lipstick, etc.
[2] *market potential*: Chances for selling.
[3] *go-ahead*: Enterprising, progressive.
[4] *initial*: First.
[5] *worthwhile*: Deserving an effort.
[6] *back us up*: Support us, give us assistance.
[7] *agreement*: Here, this means the contract document.
[8] *account sales*: Agent's statement of sales made. N.B. the phrase is singular, not plural: Account sales *has* been sent.
[9] *comprehensive range*: Wide, representative selection.
[10] *draft agreement*: Written copy of proposed contract.
[11] *household appliances*: Machines for use in the home.
[12] *keen*: Eager.
[13] *in the face of*: Against.
[14] *to step up*: To increase.
[15] *sales drive*: Sales campaign, special effort to sell goods.
[16] *gather*: To infer, note.
[17] *all-out*: Very vigorous.
[18] *taking the long view*: Looking ahead.
[19] *judicious*: Well-judged, prudent.
[20] *trade papers*: Periodicals devoted to a certain trade.
[21] *price-cut*: Reduction in price.
[22] *let competitors in*: Give competitors a chance of capturing part of the market.
[23] *seconds*: Imperfect goods offered at reduced prices.
[24] *odd*: Various, of no set design.
[25] *stipulated*: Stated as a condition.
[26] *more notice*: A longer period of warning.

## EXERCISES

1. Your firm wishes to appoint a main agent in South America for the sale of its well-known optical instruments. Write a letter to a South American distributor and offer the agency.
2. Write the South American distributor's reply.
3. A general import agent dealing with hardware goods wishes to handle an English firm's plastic ware. Write a letter for the agent making an offer of services and quoting terms.
4. Answer the letter written by the agent in no. 3 above. Accept his offer on condition that he handles no competing goods from British manufacturers.
5. Owing to rising costs in his country an export manufacturer finds he must raise his prices. Write a letter to a foreign agent asking the agent if he thinks the market will stand the proposed increases. Write also the agent's reply.
6. An import agent thinks his foreign suppliers' fixed prices too high for the market, and competitors are winning customers from him. Write to his suppliers making suggestions for reduced prices or freedom from fixed prices.
7. Send a report on market conditions from an agent to a foreign exporter. Give information on the types of goods in demand, competition and prices.
8. An export manufacturer is dissatisfied with the sales of his sole agent in a foreign country and is receiving insufficient news. Write a letter asking for action.

# 13 | Telegrams

Telegrams used to be the usual means of communication in certain types of business where a letter is too slow, and buying and selling on the *markets* or *exchanges* normally involved the sending of telegrams. Today, however, these institutions are equipped with telex machines and with direct telephone lines to foreign countries, and the importance of the telegram in such areas has been greatly reduced.

Nevertheless, not every firm can be reached by telex, and long-distance telephone calls are very expensive, so telegrams are still of very great importance in most branches of commerce.

In Britain, and in most other English-speaking countries, the word *cable* is often used for a telegram sent out of the country, whereas the term *wire* normally refers to an inland telegram. Both words can be used as nouns, verbs and adjectives: 'We have received your wire (cable)'—'You cabled (wired) us last week'—'You have not confirmed your cable (wire) reply'.

As we have already seen, firms register a *cable address* for the convenience of their business connections. This address consists of a name, usually some combination based on the name of the company itself or, if this is not possible, on the type of business carried on by the firm, followed by the name of the town. (*See example 1 on page 3*)

Telegrams are used for urgent messages, but speed must be paid for, and a good deal of skill is necessary if great expense is to be avoided. The cost depends on two factors: the distance the telegram has to travel, and the number of words it contains. It is of the greatest importance to make sure the telegram is clear, and economy often has to be sacrificed in the interests of clarity. The omission of, say, a preposition will save a few pence, but it may in certain cases result in ambiguity, and there will obviously be no saving of either time or money if the receivers have to telegraph back to find out what the message really means.

One of the characteristics of telegrams in English is that prepositions are usually left out and particles often convey the meaning of verbs. Similarly, pronouns, conjunctions and auxiliaries can be omitted provided this does not interfere with the meaning of the message. Punctuation is limited to the words 'stop' and 'query': the former is inserted at the end of a statement, the latter after a question.

Examples 1 and 2 in this chapter are suggested by letter no. 4, Chapter 3 and letter no. 4, Chapter 4 respectively.

146

[1] *Enquiry for price and delivery date*

WEATHERPROOF MANCHESTER
PLEASE QUOTE LOWEST SOONEST 250 MENS LITEWATE MEDIUM CIF
CALCUTTA—DYMONT

Note that the words *lowest* and *soonest* are used in typical cable language, which is not always correct in ordinary correspondence. They are understood to mean 'lowest price' and 'earliest delivery date'.

[2] *Reply from sellers*

DYMONT CALCUTTA
250 MENS LITEWATE MEDIUM ONETHOUSAND POUNDS CIF CALCUTTA
STOP DELIVERY THREEWEEKS FROM RECEIPT ORDER—WEATHERPROOF

Note that certain words, such as *one thousand* and *three weeks* in the example above, may be joined if they have a definite connection with each other, but this is at the discretion of the clerk who accepts the telegram.

*Further telegrams may be exchanged as follows:*

[3] PRICE TOO HIGH STOP CAN YOU REDUCE FOURPERCENT QUERY PLEASE CABLE REPLY

[4] CAN ONLY REDUCE TWOANDHALFPERCENT ON 250 OR FOURPERCENT ON 500 PLUS STOP DELIVERY AS STATED

[5] ACCEPT FOURPERCENT ON FIVEHUNDRED STOP AIRMAILING ORDER

Note that the official, written and signed order form must be sent by mail. Any telegraphic message involving orders must be confirmed.

*Here are further examples of cables relating to orders:*

[6] PREPARED PLACE IMMEDIATE ORDER PLASTICWARE SUBJECT THREEPERCENT OFF ORDER VALUE OVER ONEHUNDRED POUNDS

[7] THREEPERCENT ALLOWED ON ORDERS OVER ONEHUNDRED POUNDS CASH PAYMENT

[8] CAN ORDER THIRTYTHOUSAND MANILLA TWO ENVELOPES IF EXTRA THREEANDHALFPERCENT ALLOWED

[9] REGRET EXTRA THREEANDHALFPERCENT IMPOSSIBLE UNDER FIFTYTHOUSAND ENVELOPES STOP YOUR ORDER HELD PENDING CABLE REPLY

[10] URGENT REPEAT URGENT STOCKS RUNNING LOW PLEASE AIRFREIGHT TENTHOUSAND OFF SIX FOUR TWO BY END WEEK

[11] ORDER AIRFREIGHTED EX HEATHROW TOMORROW STOP ARRIVING MUNICH BA 956 SAMEDAY

*Inability to supply goods*

[12] REGRET UNABLE ACCEPT FURTHER ORDERS UNTIL END JUNE

[13] ORDERBOOKS FULL CANNOT GUARANTEE DELIVERY THISYEAR

[14] OWING UNCERTAIN SUPPLY POSITION UNABLE GUARANTEE DELIVERY STOP WILL CABLE DEFINITE POSITION NEXTWEEK

147

[15] UNABLE SUPPLY DXL UNTIL JUNE STOP SUGGEST INSTEAD DXM AVAILABLE FROMSTOCK STOP PLEASE CABLE REPLY

[16] OWING NEW QUOTARESTRICTIONS DELAYED EXECUTION LIKELY STOP LETTER FOLLOWS

[17] REGRET DOCKSTRIKE DELAYS SHIPMENT STOP EARLY SETTLEMENT EXPECTED BUT REQUEST ALTERNATIVE INSTRUCTIONS

## Delayed payments

[18] REGRET OWING NO NEWS FROM YOU MUST REQUEST IMMEDIATE TELEGRAPHIC REMITTANCE OR SATISFACTORY CABLE REPLY

[19] TELEGRAPHIC REPLY IMPERATIVE TO AVOID LEGAL ACTION

[20] UNLESS REPLY RECEIVED DECEMBER FIRST LATEST LEGAL ACTION UNAVOIDABLE

## Replies to nos. 18–20

[21] REMITTANCE THROUGH MIDLANDBANK TODAY STOP REGRET DELAY STOP LETTER FOLLOWS

[22] REGRET DELAY DUE TRAVELLING ABROAD STOP NATWESTBANK INSTRUCTED TRANSFER TODAY STOP LETTER FOLLOWS

[23] LETTER SENT TODAY STOP REQUEST YOU WITHHOLD ACTION

## Complaints about delivery of goods

[24] ORDER 3210 CASE TWENTYNINE RECEIVED CONTAINS DX51 NOT BX51 AS ORDERED STOP PLEASE CORRECT STOP URGENT

[25] ORDER 975 SHORTSHIPPED ONEHUNDRED KILOGRAMS PLEASE DESPATCH SOONEST

[26] IF GOODS NOT SHIPPED PLEASE AIRFREIGHT

[27] ORDER 468 CASE TWELVE ARRIVED DAMAGED STOP MAILING REPORT MEANWHILE URGENTLY REQUIRE REPLACEMENTS STOP AIRFREIGHT ESSENTIAL

[28] REGRET MV MARYBELL TOTALLOSS STOP FULL PARTICULARS FOLLOW STOP ADVISE SUPPLIERS

## Replies to complaints

[29] REGRET WRONG DELIVERY ORDER 3210 STOP ONETHOUSAND OFF BX51 ARRIVING BERLIN THURS-DAY STOP MUELLER WILL PHONE

[30] BALANCE ORDER 975 ARRIVING HAMBURG ON MV BREMERHAVEN MONDAY STOP DOCUMENTS SENT TODAY

[31] GOODS DESPATCHED FIFTEENTH ARRIVING EIGHTEENTH

[32] NEW CASE TWELVE AIRFREIGHTED TWA ARRIVING NYC NOON SATURDAY

## [33] Confirmation by letter

Dear Sirs

We confirm our telegram of yesterday's date, a copy of which is enclosed. We are also enclosing our official order no. 96832 with forwarding instructions, and look forward to receiving the consignment by the end of this month.

Yours faithfully

# EXERCISES

1. Write out telegrams 25 and 29 in full, turning them into letters. Add any information you consider necessary.
2. Do the same with telegrams 27 and 32.
3. The following cable was sent by an agent to his principal. Write out the message in full.

   US TRAVELLER OFFERING SUPERCOMPETITIVE MENSWEAR TENPERCENT UNDER YOURS STOP ESSENTIAL YOU REDUCE NOW REPEAT NOW STOP CABLE SOONEST

4. Send a cable to a customer, telling him that his order cannot be executed due to production difficulties, and offering him alternative goods from stock. Ask your customer to cable instructions.
5. Write the customer's reply.
6. You have not yet received goods ordered under no. 2541. Send a telegram to your supplier, enquiring about the whereabouts of the consignment, and pointing out that the goods are needed urgently.
7. Write a letter confirming telegram no. 21.
8. Reply by cable to telegram no. 15.
9. Write letters confirming telegrams 6 and 7.
10. Send a telegram to a business associate in London, telling him that you cannot catch the aircraft he is expecting you on. Inform him that you will be arriving on Scandinavian Airlines System flight SK 511, landing at Heathrow Airport, London, at 1015 on 27 July. Apologise for the inconvenience this last-minute change involves.

# 14 | Secretarial

The *personal assistant* or *private secretary* of an executive[1] deals with all his or her correspondence. She may be concerned with any aspect of the business of the company, but there are certain types of letters that are particularly in the province of secretaries, such as the making of appointments and travel arrangements, the writing of letters of introduction, congratulation or condolence, and invitations and replies to invitations. A secretary may also be called upon to help in the organisation of meetings and conferences and the entertainment of visiting suppliers, customers and other associates of the firm.

## RESERVING HOTEL ACCOMMODATION

[1]

We shall be glad if you will reserve the following accommodation for two of our directors, Mr Frith and Mr Collins: 2 single rooms, if possible each with a private bathroom, from 3 May, for 3 nights.

Please be so kind as to let us have an early confirmation of this booking.

[2]

The Chairman and the Managing Director of this Company will be visiting . . . in September, for the World Trade Fair, and will require a suite with two bedrooms. A single room, on the same floor if possible, will also be needed for their secretary.

Please let me know whether you can reserve this accommodation from 10 to 15 September inclusive. I shall be glad to have a reply by return, with details of your charges.

[3] *Reply to letter no. 1*

Thank you for your letter of 20 April.

I have reserved the accommodation required for your directors, Mr Frith and Mr Collins:

2 single rooms, each with a private bathroom, from 3 May, as requested.

I enclose a brochure for your further information.

[4] *This letter reserving hotel accommodation is written in a more personal tone*

Dear Mr Alleni

Mr Tredennick will be in Rome from 3 May, on a business visit, and hopes that you will be able to accommodate him again at your hotel. He will greatly appreciate it if you can let him have the same room as last year, or in any case a room at the back of the hotel, as the front rooms on the main street are rather noisy.

I shall be glad to have an early reply so that I can complete arrangements for Mr Tredennick's visit.

Yours sincerely

MARY SUGDEN

Secretary to Mr G. Tredennick

# TRAVEL ARRANGEMENTS

## [5] *Booking a seat on an aircraft*

Our Technical Director, Mr Abu Khan, will be arriving in London next week and will then go on to Sweden and Finland. We shall therefore be obliged if you will book a seat for him on a plane leaving Britain on or about the 21st, for Stockholm. Your account for the fare and booking fee will be paid by the National Bank of India, London, who have instructions to do so on our behalf.

We thank you in advance for your attention to this matter.

## [6] *Taking a car abroad*

We wish to make arrangements for the transportation of a car and four passengers from France to England, and will be glad to know what your charge is for this car-ferry service, also how much notice you require for the booking. At the same time please give us an idea of possible alternative routes and the time required for the crossing in each case.

## [7] *Reserving a berth on a ship*

Two single, first-class cabins are required for two of our directors, who will be in London next month and travelling on to New York.

The reservations are to be on the *Franconia* or the *Queen Elizabeth II*, whichever vessel is sailing about the middle of the month.

If this accommodation is not available on either ship, please let us know what alternative you can offer.

A cable reply will be appreciated.

# CORRESPONDENCE CONCERNING APPOINTMENTS

## [8]

Mr M. Peabody, our Export Manager, will be in Stockholm at the beginning of next week. He will telephone you as soon as he arrives to arrange a time for an appointment. Mr Peabody is very much looking forward to meeting you.

## [9]

I will be visiting India early next month, and will be in Bombay from the 10th until the 13th. I hope to have the pleasure of seeing you then and renewing the pleasant contact of a year ago.

## [10] *The Swedish firm replies to letter no. 8*

We thank you for your letter of 3 September and note that Mr Peabody will be in Stockholm next week. We will be delighted to see him again, and are looking forward to his telephone call.

*From the director of one firm to a director in another*

4 November 1978

B. A. Merriman Esq.
Managing Director
Pickles and Slocock Ltd.
Birmingham BI2 0BY
England

Dear Mr Merriman

In connection with the matter of a manufacturing licence,[2] I would like to have the opportunity of meeting you in person while I am in England, and would appreciate it if you could spare me an hour or two some time during the next few days. My secretary will telephone you the day after tomorrow to see when a meeting can be arranged.

Yours sincerely

*Note* the use of the addressee's name in the address and salutation, the more personal tone, and the complimentary close.

*Note* also the style of the address at the head of the letter, and remember that *Esq.*, an abbreviation of *Esquire*, is written immediately after the surname and cannot be used if you have already written *Mr*. This form of address is never used in America.

## FURTHER LETTERS ASKING FOR APPOINTMENTS

### [12]

I should much appreciate the opportunity of talking things over with you personally, as I think the various points can be settled more speedily at a meeting.

If you will suggest a time I will arrange my own appointments to fit in with yours.

### [13]

I should very much like to see you on a matter that I think will interest you, and as I shall be in Manchester next week. I hope it will be convenient for you if I call, say, on Wednesday, at 10.30 a.m., or any other time that will suit you. Perhaps you will be so kind as to let me know.

## LETTERS OF INTRODUCTION, FOR BUSINESS ASSOCIATES OF THE FIRM

### [14]

We have great pleasure in introducing to you, by this letter, Mr Mark Gillow, a director of the firm Times Flooring, Ltd., who are business associates of ours.

Mr Gillow is visiting Paris to establish new connections and we should greatly appreciate any assistance you may be able to give him, which will be considered as a personal favour to us.

[15]

It gives us great pleasure to introduce to you the bearer of this letter, Mr James Gilbert, a partner in the firm Massey, Worthington & Co. who are our accountants and auditors.

Mr Gilbert is visiting London to study the new plan on the spot, and we should be most grateful if you would give him the benefit of your advice and experience, also any introductions that may be of help to him.

Needless to say we shall regard this as a very special favour, and shall be only too pleased to reciprocate[3] if you will give us that opportunity at any time.

In the matter of introductions there is, of course, the letter given to a representative of a firm; in this case it is probable that a circular letter will be sent out also, enclosing a copy of the letter that the representative will have with him.

The following are announcements from a firm:

## [16] *Letter introducing a new Export Manager*

We have appointed Mr Arthur White to the position of Export Manager for our firm and we have given him a letter of introduction to you, which he will present when he visits Delhi in the near future. We attach a copy of the letter.

Mr White has wide experience of the markets in India and he will discuss with you the latest developments in our production methods. You may have complete confidence in his advice.

## [17] *Letter enclosed with the above*

*This will introduce to you Mr Arthur White, our new Export Manager, who is visiting our customers in Sweden.

He will tell you about our latest fabrics and will be glad to help you with any technical information you may require.

* *Or*: The bearer of this letter is Mr A. White . . .

In reply to the above the following could be written:

[18]

We shall be very glad to see your new Export Manager when he is in this country, and we hope he will take an early opportunity to pay us a visit.

Representatives[4] may also be sent to visit customers or suppliers in connection with offers—or complaints:

## [19] *Announcing the visit of a representative of the firm for purposes of inspection*

As our Export Manager is now in Europe and will be visiting Spain next month (we have written to ask him) (we have telegraphed to him) to get in touch with you and arrange to inspect the goods at your warehouse.

[20]

Mr Greening, who is our Buyer[5] for Europe, will visit your warehouse and inspect the goods as soon as he arrives.

# LETTERS OF CONGRATULATION

From the purely business angle a letter of congratulation is often required; an executive of a firm may have received some honour, or attained an important position, and should be congratulated.

It is important to remember that in Britain honours are conferred by the Sovereign twice a year, at the New Year and at the time of the Sovereign's official birthday in June. There are a good many business people among the recipients of such honours, which are given for services to the country.

The following are suitable phrases for such letters:

1. It was with great pleasure that we learnt of (your appointment) (your success) . . .
2. May we congratulate you on (your appointment) (your success) . . .
3. We wish to express our great pleasure on hearing of your . . .
4. It was with great pleasure that we read in the papers that you had received the . . . (*name of honour conferred*) and we want to congratulate you at once.
5. We were delighted to read in the papers that you had received the . . .
6. We should like to say that we feel it is a fitting reward for your work.
7. May we say that we think no one has done more to deserve this reward.
8. We want to send you our very good wishes.
9. May we express our sincere good wishes.

# LETTERS OF SYMPATHY, CONDOLENCE

These are usually called for on the death of an executive of another firm; they are always difficult letters to write and much depends on how well the sympathisers know the people they are writing to. Again, such letters can be written from the angle of business rather than personal association.

It is not the custom in Britain to send out long announcements of deaths. A notice is put in the appropriate column of such papers as *The Times*, and in the case of companies the Chairman, in his report for the annual general meeting of shareholders, mentions the death or retirement of any members of the Board of Directors. However, letters would be written to regular business associates and especially to any who knew the director personally.

Something on the following lines would be written by the Secretary of the company:

[21] *Letter announcing the death of a Chairman*

You will, I know, be very sorry to hear of the sudden death of Sir James Brown, for thirty years Chairman of this company and a son of the founder of the business . . .

The following phrases would be suitable for the reply expressing sympathy:

10. We were deeply grieved (to hear) (to learn) of the sudden death of the Chairman of your company . . .
11. It was a great shock to hear the sad news of Sir James Brown's sudden death.
12. We are writing immediately to express our sincere sympathy.
13. We want to express our heartfelt sympathy . . .
14. All who knew him well remember his many kindnesses and his helpful advice.
15. Please (convey) (express) our sympathy also to his family.

A rather formal phrase is:

16. Please accept the expression of our deepest sympathy.


## INVITATIONS

There are many occasions on which firms issue invitations, as do societies of various kinds. There are social gatherings for the members of the staff, especially during the Christmas and New Year season, and there are also official banquets as well as other activities.

The invitation is a formal one and printed cards are sent, usually with the following wording:

[22]

---

# The Chairman and Directors of Marjoy Ltd.

*request the pleasure of your company at a Banquet to be held at the Great Hall, Western Avenue, Bournemouth at 8.30 p.m. on Friday, 20th October, 1978.*

*Evening Dress*

*R.S.V.P.*
*to the Secretary.*

---

R.S.V.P. (= 'Répondez s'il vous plaît') is always printed on such formal invitations; the wording on the left ensures that full 'evening dress' is worn by everyone. Sometimes wording on the left indicates the type of 'entertainment' provided for the guests; when this is done the wording such as 'at a Banquet to be held' would be omitted. As an example, meetings are frequently organised for the early evening, between 6 and 8 o'clock, and in the bottom left-hand corner the word 'Cocktails' is printed.

The name of the company may be left out and printed at the top, or the bottom of the card.

The answer to such formal invitations is in the third person; the guest uses notepaper with the address already die-stamped[6] at the head, or writes in his address, but no name and address of the firm appears, neither is the salutation 'Dear Sirs' used nor the ending 'Yours faithfully'. In fact the reply would look like this:

[23]

> 30 Ferndale Road
> Bournemouth
>
> Mr John Smith thanks The Chairman and Directors of Marjoy Ltd. for their kind invitation to a Banquet to be held at the Great Hall, Western Avenue, Bournemouth at 8.30 p.m. on Friday, 20th October, 1978, which he has much pleasure in accepting.

(There is no signature to this letter.)

If Mr John Smith is obliged to refuse the invitation, the wording of the last two lines would be: '. . . but regrets that he is unable to accept owing to a prior engagement on that (day) (evening).'

Informal, personal invitations are, of course, written and answered in the same way as other private correspondence.

## HOSPITALITY

[24] *A letter from an overseas customer, announcing a visit. (Note that the letter is written in the American style.)*

Gentlemen:

We have the pleasure to announce that our Technical Director, Mr Daly, is planning to visit you early in October next, the purpose of which visit will be to study on the spot,[7] with your valuable assistance and co-operation, various questions of importance, including of course our joint program for research.

It will be very helpful for him to exchange ideas about the promotion of the business, and meetings could perhaps be arranged with various authorities who may be interested in the constructional projects we have in view. Your kind suggestions will be highly appreciated.

You will be informed in advance of the exact day on which Mr Daly will arrive in England. Meanwhile, with kind regards to your Directors, we are

Very truly yours

When he returns to his own country, after the visit proposed in the above letter, Mr Daly will write a letter of thanks for the hospitality received. This can be an official letter from his firm but a much more personal and friendly letter can be written, on the following lines:

[25] *A letter of thanks for hospitality (See letter no. 24)*

(Private address of the American writer,
    or the address of his office
    but without the firm's name.)

                                                                8 June 1978

Sir Walter Drake K.C.M.G.
Chairman
The Drake & Sons Engineering Co. Ltd.
BRISTOL 5
England

Dear Sir Walter

Back now in my own country I wish to thank you most warmly for your very excellent hospitality extended to me. The opportunity to meet yourself and your directors is something I had long looked forward to, and I can only hope now that one day I may be able to receive a visit here from you.

I very much appreciated your kindness and that of Mr James Frobisher in showing me round the new plant.

I thank you once again, and am,

Sincerely

J. DALY

(A more formal letter of thanks could be addressed to the Secretary of the company, asking him 'to convey' the thanks of the writer to the Chairman and directors.)

## THE COMPANY SECRETARY

As stated in Chapter 2 all limited companies are required, under British Company Law, to have a *Company Secretary*; in the case of private companies the directors are free to appoint any suitable person for this position, but in the case of public companies—where the money of the public is concerned—the Company Secretary must be a properly qualified person, a member of a recognised Institute or Association.

The correspondence of the Company Secretary is particulary concerned with shareholders' meetings, board meetings, and the various forms that must be sent in to the office of the Registrar of Joint Stock Companies (the Government department concerned with company regulations).

The Company Secretary may also deal with enquiries for information concerning other firms, although the Accounts Department often handles these matters. Administrative questions outside the ordinary trading come into the sphere of the Company Secretary, under instructions of the Board of Directors.

*The Company Secretary writes to the Chairman of the Board of Directors*
17.  I think it would be advisable to call a meeting to discuss the matter of . . .* that has just arisen. If you will kindly let me know a day and time suitable to you I will then contact the other members of the Board.

* The matter to be discussed could be: price reductions; employees' pensions; or a 'take-over bid'.[8]

*Further phrasing for letters written by a Company Secretary, for the Chairman of a company*
18.  The Chairman has asked me to call a round-table meeting,[9] to discuss the take-over bid with the other parties interested.
19.  The Chairman has instructed me to say that he considers it advisable to call a meeting at an early date.
20.  In view of the difficulties that have arisen I think it is advisable to call a meeting, so that the whole matter can be thrashed out.[10]
21.  I feel these matters can be more speedily settled at a meeting.

*Official phrasing used by the Company Secretary when writing letters either to directors or to shareholders, or other persons concerned*
22.  The Chairman has asked me (to write to you) (to inform you) . . .
23.  I have been instructed by the Board . . .
24.  I have been requested (by the Chairman) (by the Board) . . .
25.  At the request (of the Chairman) (of the Board) I am writing . . .

158

26. As requested, I am enclosing a copy of the Minutes of the last meeting, concerning . . .

27. . . . I am enclosing a copy of the resolution passed at the last meeting of the Board . . .

## LEGAL MATTERS

In the case of small firms various matters are dealt with by the Secretary on the instructions of, and after discussion with, the directors; in larger firms these matters would be the concern of the Accounts Department, in other words of the Chief Accountant, or Accountant, also after discussion with the directors. Among such matters would be any legal action to be taken in the case of non-payment of debt, default in carrying out a contract, or a dispute of any kind involving the firm.

The directors of a company do not act without the advice of the company's solicitors, and all contracts and agreements entered into are first approved by the lawyers.

It is sometimes necessary to ask solicitors in another country to act on the firm's behalf, and the following type of letter might then be written:

[26] *Letter to solicitors, asking them to act for the firm*

Your name has been given to us by Green, Black & Green,* our solicitors in Luton, and I am writing at the request of my Directors to ask if you would be good enough to act on our behalf in the matter of non-fulfilment of a contract by . . . (*name given*) of your city. The precise facts of the case are set out in the enclosed copy of the document and attached statement by my Directors.

We hope you will be willing to undertake the case for our company, and as the matter is rather urgent your early reply will be greatly appreciated.

(This letter would be signed by the Secretary of the company.)

* The name of the solicitors might also be obtained from the Embassy of the country in which the legal action will be brought, or from the Board of Trade in London, etc.

## INVESTMENTS

Like a private individual, a firm invests that part of its funds which are not immediately required for necessary payments, and like an individual, the firm usually buys shares or stock on the Stock Exchange.

The very large organisations, such as the banks and insurance companies, are big shareholders in other concerns.

A company cannot buy its own shares.

This investment of funds is a matter for the Board of Directors, and again the Company Secretary as well as the Accountant of the firm are concerned.

The enquiries are usually made and instructions given by telephone but the brokers will confirm the transaction by the sending of contract notes, either for buying or selling.

159

The following are examples of phrases used in correspondence on this matter:

## Buying and selling on the Stock Exchange

28.  We confirm our telephone conversation and shall be glad if you will buy on our behalf the following shares and government bonds:
29.  We confirm our telegram of today, instructing you to buy for our account: 500 ordinary shares in . . . (*name of firm*). As the market in these shares is decidedly dull at present we hope that you can get them at a very reasonable price.

## Broker's replies to instructions

30.  We are pleased to advise you that, in accordance with your instructions, we have this day BOUGHT, for settlement cash, the following: . . .
31.  We have received your letter of yesterday, confirming your telegram, and in accordance with your instructions we SOLD your *holding* [11] of . . . (*number and type of shares*) in . . . (*name of firm*). The contract note, giving details of this transaction, is enclosed and the proceeds of the sale will be credited to your account in due course.
32.  With reference to your recent call at our office, we now enclose a memorandum giving an opinion on your investments, together with suggestions for the investment of the other funds you have available. We shall be happy to supply you with any further information you may require, and to carry out any changes on which you may decide.
33.  We confirm the receipt of your instructions to sell: 755 Ordinary VICKERS *at best*.[12] This order will be considered in force until completed or cancelled.
34.  We have remitted the sum of . . ., representing the sale proceeds[13] of the securities on . . . (*date given*) to the Bank of . . ., for your credit, as instructed.

Instead of dealing direct with brokers a firm may buy and sell shares through its bank; the bank employs the services of a broker to buy and sell on the Stock Exchange and the commission is shared. The following are examples of correspondence with a bank for the buying of shares.

## [27] *Instructions to a bank to purchase shares*

THE WESTERN TRADING COMPANY LTD. PLYMOUTH

The Manager                                                              3 January 1978
Bank of Commerce Ltd.
Plymouth PL2 4CF

Dear Sir

In confirmation of our telephone instructions of this morning, will you please arrange for the purchase of the following shares for my company at best:

1,000 Ordinary, Great Union Steel, @ about 150
 500 Preference, Western Plastics, @ about 175

Our cheque to cover the purchase price will be forwarded to you immediately upon receipt of your advice of completed purchase. Will you please meanwhile send me the contract notes and documents authorising the companies to pay the dividends to you for the credit of the Western Trading Company.

The share certificates should be forwarded to me in due course.

Yours faithfully

THE WESTERN TRADING CO. LTD.
Secretary

160

## BANK OF COMMERCE LTD.

## PLYMOUTH

5 January 1978

The Secretary
The Western Trading Co. Ltd.
PLYMOUTH PL2 9DH

Dear Sir

In accordance with the instructions contained in your letter of
3 January, we have obtained the following shares for your company:

1,000 Ordinary Grand Union Steel, @ 153
  500 Preference Western Plastics, @ 172

The contract notes are enclosed, together with the forms authorising
the payment of dividends to this bank. We shall be glad if you will
sign the latter and return the forms to us.

We have noted your instructions regarding crediting of dividends
and forwarding of share certificates.

As you will see from the contract notes, the total amount due to
us in respect of these transactions is £2,390, including our
charges and stamp duty, and we should be glad to have your
cheque for this amount.

Yours faithfully
BANK OF COMMERCE LTD.

*F. Books.*

Manager

## GLOSSARY OF TERMS

*Association*: An organisation that protects the interests of its members
but does not trade.

*Corporation*: A large organisation, particularly in the U.S.A.; a munici-
pal enterprise.

*Society*: This name is not generally used in Britain for commercial firms,
but for cultural, charitable and such organisations.

*Explanation of reference numbers in this chapter*

[1] *executive*: This name is now applied to any director, manager or other person in authority, in the business of a firm.

[2] *manufacturing licence*: It is the custom of manufacturers to grant a permit, or licence, to similar firms in other countries, to manufacture the products, using the trade mark of the first manufacturers but not their name.

[3] *reciprocate*: Render the same service (in introductions, as in reference enquiries, it is considered polite to offer to return the service, or favour, at some time).

[4] *representative*: The person or firm appointed as an agent or distributor but also anyone representing the firm, such as: travelling salesman, manager or director.

[5] *buyer*: A name specially used in British trading for the purchases or buying manager. The *buyer* is in control of all purchases made by the firm for re-sale.

[6] *die-stamping*: This is used for addresses on private notepaper; it is not printed but *embossed* and usually coloured.

[7] *on the spot*: In the place where the goods are made.

[8] *'take-over bid'*: This is an offer, usually from another firm, to take over the business of the company concerned; it may be by amalgamation or absorption. The purchase of a certain number of Ordinary shares in a company gives a 'controlling interest'.

[9] *'round-table' meeting*: This usually means that the participants meet on equal terms (the expression probably originated with the Round Table of the legendary King Arthur and his knights, at which nobody had precedence over another).

[10] *'thrashed out'*: Discussed and argued over until some decision is reached (the word, like 'thresh' comes from the beating of corn to extract the grain).

*Stock Exchange and bank terms*

[11] *holding*: The shares are said to be 'held' by the owner, who is a shareholder, or stockholder.

[12] *'at best'*: At the best possible price that can be obtained.

[13] *proceeds*: The result of the sale represented in money (this word is generally used by banks for the money they collect on cheques, bills of exchange, etc.).

## EXERCISES

1. Write to an airline, booking seats for an executive who is about to travel from your city to London, where he will be staying for five days, and from there to New York. He will be returning after a week in New York.

2. Arrange hotel accommodation in London for the same executive.
3. Inform your company's associates in Madrid that your Marketing Manager will be visiting customers in Spain next month, and attempt to arrange an appointment for him.
4. Write a reply to the letter in exercise 3.
5. Using the following notes, write a letter to a Japanese company, introducing the person mentioned:
   introduce—Stephen Hampden—director—Avex Ltd.—associates. —visiting Tokyo—exploring market potential—grateful help—glad to reciprocate.
6. On behalf of your Board of Directors, issue a formal invitation to a cocktail party at the Henderson Building, 28 Soho Square, London WC1, on 24 May this year at 6 p.m.
7. Write two replies to the invitation in exercise 6, one accepting and the other refusing.
8. You have just returned from a three-day visit to an overseas supplier. Write a letter thanking your hosts for their hospitality.